DESIGNATED HEROES REMEMBER

DESIGNATED HEROES REMEMBER

World War II Survivors
Americans — Germans
Civilians — Military
Christians — Jews

Tell Their Stories
1933 — 1945

Edited by Sheila Dineen Jordan — Leo Bach
Patricia Mills — Joelie Pehanick

Published by
The Write Way Publishing Company
Walnut Creek, California

DESIGNATED HEROES REMEMBER

World War II Survivors
Americans — Germans
Civilians — Military —Christians — Jews
Tell Their Stories
1933 — 1945

The Write Way Publishing Company
Books may be ordered through your bookseller

ISBN 978-0-9774689-1-1

Printed in the United States of America

2224 Pine Knoll Drive, Suite One
Walnut Creek, CA 94595
(925) 937-7313

Table of Contents

INTRODUCTION
Sheila Dineen Jordan

This book, instead of the story of millions of deaths, is the story of one survivor at a time. Somehow, reading about one thirteen-year-old, or a mom and dad, a nephew, a baby, — somehow that tears at the heart and forces one to remember the horrors for a much longer time. In history class, the subject of six million Jews slaughtered registers in the mind as a terrible thing, but it does not register in the soul.

We are in a writing class where many of the survivors of that terrible time in history are writing their memories. Sometimes they write to share with their families, but mostly to exorcize the demons that have haunted their dreams for more than sixty years. As we have listened to these stories, we've had our own dreams of these tales and have been haunted by them. These accounts encompass many nationalities: Germans, Americans, English, Filipino, Japanese and many Jews. It is apparent that all sides faced such horror, the innocent young men and women, the children. If these stories touch one's soul, perhaps there is hope for this battered, banged up, but still beautiful planet.

ACKNOWLEDGMENTS

Mary Webb, mentor, teacher, friend to each and every author in this book.

Lee Donehower, who so generously performed his technical magic and presented us with a worthy collaborative effort.

Caroline Van Remortel, graphic artist extraordinaire, who took a partially designed book cover into her talented hands and fashioned it into a winner.

To those who did not survive

The
Authors

Leo Bach
Shirley Barshay
Sarah Connelly
John Cline
Irmhild Epstein
Susan Hochschild
Helen Knopp
Peter Kunkel
Milton Matz
Leonard Morgenstern
Joelie Pehanick
Steffi Plumb
Sylvia Rose
Otto Schnepp
Eileen Schnepp
Jules Schwartz
Helmut Unbehoven
Frank Weinman
Adrienne Wolfert
Ruth Roque-Wood

About The Authors

From silversmith to 60's radical, from medical internist to German teacher, from corporate attorney to pastoral psychologist – so goes a smattering of the backgrounds of *Designated Heroes Remember*. They are sixty something to ninety plus in calendar years and off the charts in wisdom and grace, these Rossmoor writers. Most are transplants from other states — or countries, with English as their second, third or more language. In those cases their work was only edited for clarity, the foreign flavor retained. Three have passed on, leaving their 'war words' to grateful readers and posterity.

Some were writing and sharing profusely with the group for years – the very reason this book was conceived. Others had buried "those times" with finality — until this book was conceived. All were amazed at what vivid memories, what minute details bobbed to the surface when they began putting thoughts to words, then words to paper. And it wasn't only prose that poured forth — so did a play, a poem, an interview. Still, after over sixty years, they concede that some particulars stay dim, some numbers may not be totally accurate. But each selection is as best the author can recall it, though that recollection may clash with another's who was also present.

In many cases their writing earned the gratefulness of their offspring who, until now, had only heard hazy references to their parent's early life or amusing anecdotes or nothing at all. But the process was often painful — akin to that of drilling out a deep cavity without Novocain. Simultaneously, it proved to be cathartic for some. Most of the authors were boys and girls when their lives helplessly exploded. Within months, weeks, even days, childhoods vanished; they had to be men and women.

The substance of these written pages helped mold their very beings, fortified their characters and made them the insightful and captivating adults that they are today. That is their most significant commonality.

EDITOR'S NOTE: Rossmoor is a retirement community of some ten thousand people in the San Francisco Bay Area. The Writer's Group is one of over a hundred organizations within the community.

 *PETER KUNKEL'S innate sensibilities command your attention and capture your heart whether in conversation or in his written word. Through the eyes of the boy he was, he shares, with clarity and wisdom beyond his years, what it was like growing up in Hitler's Germany in the 1930s and his solo immigration to freedom and safety in the United States. He was the eldest of three children born to a beloved Jewish mother and a Gentile father.*

THE VISIT

JANUARY TO MAY, 1933,
WHEN I TURNED 12

During breakfast on the last Sunday in January, Vati (Daddy) said: "We haven't been to the Zeughaus Museum for a long time. How would you like to go there this afternoon?"

I said, "Yes, I want to go again." Nodding at Vati's missing arm, I added, "I hate what happened to you during the war. I hate what weapons do, but still I want to look at them. I feel bewitched."

From the way Vati looked at me, I could tell he understood. "You know, the first human beings had primitive weapons for hunting and fighting off animals that wanted to eat them."

"Ja," I said, "in the Zeughaus I saw arrowheads made of stone."

"Thousands of years later there were many more people on the earth," replied Vati. "Family groups had grown into tribes, and tribes began to own land. Warfare began when they had to defend their land against other tribes. That's when special tools were invented for killing people."

I admired the way Vati could talk like that with his missing arm, as if what he was saying had nothing to do with him.

"I want to go, too," said my brother, Wulf. "But I don't care about the weapons. What interests me are the walls and fortresses that were built to keep out the armies that did the killing."

§

We had been in the Zeughaus about two hours when it began to get dark. The uniformed man in charge of the room switched on the huge chandelier that hung in the middle of the ceiling, flooding everything with light. Looking up, I was amazed that all that brightness came from many little light bulbs that were made to look just like candles.

When Vati could tell that Wulf and I were getting tired, he said, "Before we go to the pastry shop across the street, let me show you something in the Hall of Knights next door."

Ignoring all the other exhibits, he took us to the standing figure of a knight in full armor. His shiny breastplate had a hole in it as big as a fist. Vati said, "That hole was made by a musket ball." After a pause he added, "When a common soldier with a musket could kill a noble knight, knights became useless."

That gave me an awful feeling in my belly. "Vati, I loved the stories you read to us about Siegfried and the Knights of the Round Table. I don't like that they were wiped out by those stupid muskets."

Vati had a little smile on his face when he said, "It is a fact that knights were killed by muskets. But the ancient stories will survive as long as people like to tell them."

Next evening Vati came to supper looking upset. He took the *Berliner Tageblatt* out from under his arm and showed us the front page. In large black letters we saw END OF WEIMAR REPUBLIC.

Then he said, "President von Hinderburg made Hitler Chancellor and suspended the Weimar constitution. From now on, Germany will be governed by the cabinet which is supposed to include members of all of the major parties. But I don't trust Hitler."

"Mein Gott," said Mutter. "I thought President von Hinderburg despised Hitler and his rowdy Brown Shirts. How could he appoint him Chancellor?"

"Hinderburg made no public statement, but he and his main advisor, von Papen, are aristocrats. They are monarchists and distrust democracy. I think Hinderburg actually believes communism and socialism are a bigger threat to Germany than fascism."

I didn't like that Vati and Mutter looked unhappy, but even when Mutti was still alive, it often happened that she and Vati worried about stuff that didn't bother us kids at all.

For me, life went on as usual. I loved going to school and learning new things all the time. But I thought it was strange that Heinz Schmincke had changed from talking all the time to being quiet. I didn't like him either way, but quiet was better. One day when we were riding home on the U-Bahn, he said, "My dad is in a bad mood. He thinks Hitler won't be satisfied until he is dictator. He already made Göering Minister of the Interior of Prussia, giving him command of the police of the whole province."

On the last Monday evening in February, one month after Hitler became Chancellor, a terrible thing happened. We heard fire engines and police cars racing down our street towards the center of the city. From our balcony we could see far away to where the Brandenburger Gate was and the glow of a big fire that made the clouds look orange.

The next evening Vati told us, "The *Tageblatt* reports last night's fire was in the Reichstag and was deliberately set. Police and firemen are said to have seen a man running around in the burning building, setting furniture on fire. When they arrested him, they found a Dutch passport and a communist party membership card in his pocket. His name is Van der Lubbe."

Then Vati turned to the third page and said, "Let me read you the beginning of this special article by one of their top reporters. 'Before dawn this morning, Göering ordered the police to arrest all communist delegates to the Reichstag, stating that the fire was a communist conspiracy.'"

Then he sat quietly with a faraway look on his face as if he could see right through the wall across from him. Finally he said, "I think Van der Lubbe was brought up there by the Storm Troopers. If he had planned to start a fire on his own, he would not have had his Dutch passport and communist membership card with him."

Then he leaned forward, looked at each of us in the eyes for a moment and said, "You must not tell anyone about this conversation. And never talk about this among yourselves outside this room."

Mutter was upset.

"Fritz, you are frightening the children."

Vati looked at her and said firmly, "Elizabeth, we have to be very careful from now on. I think this is part of Hitler's scheme."

I don't know why, but what Vati said reminded me of the big hole in the knight's armor, and I was scared. The next day Heinz Schmincke was not in school. I was glad my dad was not a communist delegate. Although I was more afraid than ever, I decided to be brave and to pretend that everything was all right.

Two days after the fire, Vati looked very troubled when he came to breakfast with the *Berliner Tageblatt* under his arm. When Mutter saw his face, she said, "Mein Gott, more bad news?"

Holding up the paper, he said, "The front page now has a section for announcements and decrees. The text comes directly from Göebbels' office. Today it says, 'In order to give Chancellor Hitler sufficient power to fight the communist revolution, President von Hinderburg suspended, for a period of three years, the civil rights guaranteed by the constitution.'"

Mutter said, "But, Fritz, do you think law-abiding citizens will have to worry about that?"

"Elizabeth, it means the police can enter anybody's home at any time without a warrant, search and confiscate property and arrest people without telling them why."

Mutter was angry. "I don't think it is right to frighten the children with this kind of talk."

With a grim expression on his face, Vati said in a low voice, "There are times when fear can save our lives because it makes us more careful."

While we were having breakfast together on Easter Sunday and my baby brother, Jochi, was sleeping peacefully in his basket on the floor between Mia and Mutter, Vati, looking at Wulf and me, said, "Before we go to see our new boat in Falkensee, I want to have a talk with both of you in my study."

When we were settled on the sofa across from his desk, he asked, "Did Amo (grandmother) or Onkel (uncle) Manfred ever mention to you that they are Jewish?" We both shook our heads. Vati's face looked serious but calm. I felt like throwing up.

"Nobody in the Lowengard family ever thought of themselves as Jewish. As far as I know, they are all atheists. Your mother certainly was. But for Hitler, Jewishness is a matter of race rather than religion. Since Hinderburg suspended civil rights, Hitler has issued a lot of decrees against Jews."

Vati paused and a slight smile crept into his eyes and mouth. "For you, what matters is that you will not be allowed to study at a university in Germany. And I don't think you would want to after all the Jewish professors have been dismissed."

Wulf said, "With our blond hair and the last name Kunkel, how can anybody tell we are Jewish? We definitely look less Jewish than Herr Göebbels." Vati and I laughed and Wulf looked pleased.

Vati continued, "When Douglas Steere visited me last month, he told me the Quakers are setting up a boarding school in Holland for children who have to leave Germany. Students will learn English and be taught what they need to know to pass the Oxford University entrance examination. With what is called the Oxford matriculation certificate, they will be accepted by any English speaking university in the world." With a big smile he added, "In your case, that will be in America."

ॐ

One afternoon in the middle of May, I was playing with Jochi on the dining room floor. He had discovered that he could crawl over to a chair, pull himself up and stand for a few seconds before plopping down on the pillow of diapers Mutter had strapped to his bottom. Both of us were giggling.

When Mutter came in from the kitchen, she smiled and said, "You two look like you are having fun." Then she added, "Peter, tomorrow, right after breakfast, Vati and I are going to take Jochi to Dr. Samson for his checkup. We will leave you in charge. If the telephone rings, don't answer it. If the doorbell rings, it will probably be the mailman. Vati is expecting a registered letter."

The next afternoon I was curled up in my favorite chair in the dining room, reading *Huckleberry Finn*. When the doorbell rang I thought it was the mailman. I was terrified when I opened the door and saw Heinz Schmincke standing there with a man I took to be his father. They both looked awful and smelled worse.

"May we come in?" asked the father in a cracked voice. My insides turned to ice as I recalled what I had heard about concentration camps and the Gestapo while listening to Onkel Hans talking to Vati the last time he was here.

"No," I said. "My parents are not here. I am not supposed to let anybody in." They came in anyway, all the way into the living room. Looking around with hungry eyes, the father touched the backs of the upholstered chairs as if they reminded him of what was once his home.

"You have to leave," I said. "My parents are not here. Please leave."

"When are they coming home?" asked the father.

"I don't know. They said late. But you must leave now. My parents are not here."

"We could wait here for them," said the father.

"No, you must leave now. I am not allowed to let you stay."

Now the ice melted in my belly and my heart began to pound. I started to sweat. Then I walked up to Heinz. Close to his face, I said in a loud voice, "Look, my parents are not here. They are coming home late. You must go."

Father and son looked at each other with despair, turned and left without another word. When I had closed the door behind them I fell into the nearest chair and wept for a long time. I was not just sad. I never knew tears had so much to say.

Vati and Mutter came home about an hour later. Jochi was crying because he was hungry, and Mutter went off to feed him. When I told Vati what had happened, I started to cry again. He put his arm on my shoulder and said, "You did the right thing. There is no way we could have saved them. And if the Gestapo had found them here, our whole family might have perished. Thank you for what you did." He held me with his arm around my shoulder until I stopped crying.

THE CROSSING

OCTOBER AND NOVEMBER, 1938, AGE 17

(Note: After graduating from the Quaker school in Holland, Peter went to Berlin for a visit and then returned to the school before leaving for America. Peter's nickname at the school was Palma.)

I got back from Berlin in the afternoon of Monday, October 17, 1938, haunted by what had happened at the border with the Gestapo. Even though everything was peaceful here, I didn't feel safe. At home we could always talk with Vati when something upset us. Here, I liked to see Frau Einstein, our housemother. Students could usually talk with her in the afternoon.

When I arrived in the waiting room, there was a notice on the door to her office: FAMILY CONFERENCE: DO NOT DISTURB. I sat down to wait. Through a small window in the door to her office she could see me sitting there.

After awhile she came out and said, "Palma, I won't be able to see you this afternoon, but since summer vacation has started, could you come back after breakfast tomorrow?"

"Oh, thanks. I would like that. I don't know what's the matter with me. I'm so tired that I would rather sleep than eat." As I was walking back to my room looking forward to my nap, I heard the opening bars of Mozart's *Oboe Quartet* in my head. I had that record on the gramophone in my room and drifted off to sleep with the jubilant music whispering gently in my ear. When I woke up an hour later, I was rested and hungry.

The dining room was set up with tables for ten, each headed by a teacher. Most classes were small enough so that we could all eat together. At the head of our table sat Miss Green. In Quaker fashion, we began each meal joining hands for a few minutes of silence. The peacefulness of that moment made me so grateful to be there that tears came into my eyes. I was glad my two friends, Peter Grunthal and Ruth Enouch, were sitting across from me because I wanted to tell somebody what I had gone through this afternoon.

I said, "I know I am safe here, but I won't get rid of the fear in my belly 'til I am aboard the *Veendam* in Southampton three weeks from now."

Ruth had a puzzled look on her face. "What's the matter with you, Palma? Tears in your eyes a moment ago and now fear in your belly?"

"Well, I had trouble with the Gestapo yesterday when I was on my way back from Berlin."

Peter interrupted, "You went to Berlin? Are you crazy?"

"No, I have been going back and forth a lot. With a German passport and a German last name, no one can tell we had a Jewish mother, and as Wulf pointed out some time ago, with blond hair and blue eyes I don't look nearly as Jewish as Herr Göebbels."

"So how did the Gestapo get into this story?" asked Peter.

"Change in policy. Over this past weekend the Gestapo took over the passport control at the Dutch border. The officer asked me why an able bodied young man was leaving Germany when der Führer needs him. I followed my father's instructions and told him I was going to school in Holland to learn English. The officer was gone a long time, and I was really scared, but when he came back he smiled at me. Apparently my learning English fits in with the Füher's plans." I paused, then added, "It's too bad Holland America Line no longer uses Rotterdam."

Peter said, "I, too, would prefer to leave from Rotterdam. The worst part about this trip is that after the night on the ferry, it takes the whole next day on what they call 'Boat Trains' to get from Harwich to Southampton. My father became a U.S. citizen last year, so the American consul in Rotterdam gave me a visa right away. As soon as I found out we had all passed the Oxford Matriculation examination, I cabled Dad and he sent me a second class ticket on the *USS Washington*. It leaves Southampton on Saturday the 22nd. Passengers are supposed to board the night before, so I have to leave here after lunch, day after tomorrow."

"Man, am I glad we had this conversation," I said. "I had no idea it took that long to get to Southampton."

When I went to see Frau Einstein the next morning she said, "You look as if you're feeling better."

"I'm not tired any more, but I still have an awful feeling in my belly as if I had swallowed a rock."

"Well, why don't you tell me what happened yesterday at the border?" While listening to my story she never took her calm brown eyes off me. They reminded me of Mutti.

When I finished she looked at me for a long time in silence. The expression on her face made me feel she saw more about what was going on in me than I could see myself. Then she asked, "Had you ever thought before that you might die?"

As she said that, sobs rose from deep inside me. The calm and caring way she looked at me told me that crying was all right. I wept for a long time and felt the rock in my belly melting away.

When my tears stopped flowing, she smiled at me and said in a gentle voice, "Palma, this is the end of your childhood. You are now a young man. Have fun. Take good care of yourself and be gentle. Life is precious and fragile."

"Thank you, Frau Einstein. This is like magic. Suddenly I feel wonderful."

She laughed and said, "What happened here this morning is done by both of us. I wish you a good journey."

Somehow I knew she didn't mean just my trip to America but my whole life's journey.

Back in my room I sat down to write a letter to my father. When I saw that the first two words I had written automatically were "Dear Vati," I realized that it no longer felt right. It was time to change to Vater. In the letter I told him how long it took to get from Eerde to Southampton, and that I would need some money for tipping and travel expenses. In his response he reassured me that once I got to Haverford I would not have to worry about money, because Tante Lowengard had made arrangements through her bank for a monthly transfer for tuition as well as room and board. In the letter was a 200 mark note for travel money.

After lunch on Friday, November 11, Herr Reckendorf, my teacher, drove me to Zwolle in the school's old Fiat. My only baggage was one small suitcase.

While we were waiting for the bus to the Hook of Holland, he said, "I understand Jurgen is going to meet you when you land in New York. Give him my regards and tell him to write to us. We always wonder how our former students are doing." Then he smiled and added, "The same goes for you, of course."

"I wonder myself how I'll get along in America," I said. "I probably won't write until I've been there awhile."

When my bus arrived we shook hands, and I said, "Thank you for being such a good teacher. I learned a lot from you."

"Palma," he said, "you are a good student, but don't forget to play and enjoy yourself."

"Frau Einstein told me the same thing, and Ruth Enoch said I was too serious and too hard on myself. How can I help being the way I am? Do you want me to be real serious about playing?"

He laughed. "None of us wants you to make an effort. Just relax and be yourself. I wish you a good journey."

I climbed aboard and waved to him from my window seat. As the bus began to move away, I heard Frau Einstein's voice in my head, "Palma, this is the end of your childhood." That had felt good in her caring presence, but now, knowing I was really alone, my mood turned dark.

Engrossed in reading *The Book of San Michele*, I did not see the Dutch countryside glide by. When the driver announced, "Hook of Holland, the ferry leaves in two hours," I was amazed to see so many people and cars already lined up to board. Against the background of a beautiful sunset the huge ferry cast a black shadow over the dock. There were two lines. I joined the longer one and found myself standing behind a woman with two children who were speaking English with a German accent. I asked her in German how much the fare was. My being young and alone must have aroused some motherly feelings, and my small suitcase probably identified me as a refugee. She pointed to the other line of people and said in English, "They will sell you a ticket if you show them a passport, a visa, and proof that you have passage to America. They accept guilders, British pounds, and Deutsche marks. The price depends on what accommodations you buy. The cheapest is a seat in the lounge. That costs 50 guilders."

In the lounge I found a chair under a lamp. It was a strange feeling to sleep in the same room with so many people and to listen to the music of their snores and soft voices with the throbbing of the engine in the background. Throughout the night I drifted back and forth between sleep and *The Book of San Michele.*

At 6:00 a.m. a voice came over the loudspeaker, "We will be docking in Harwich in about one hour. For passengers going on to Southampton, the first boat train leaves Harwich at 8:30."

Man, was I hungry. Thinking, when in Rome do as the Romans do, I had fish and chips. It filled me up and was also the cheapest, but the taste reminded me that salt is an English cook's favorite spice.

It was late afternoon when I, along with a tired and bedraggled looking bunch of passengers, arrived at the dock where the *Veendam* was moored. A friendly English speaking Dutchman checked my papers and turned me over to a member of the crew who took my suitcase and said, "Follow me."

We climbed a set of stairs from the dock to the main deck. Then we went way down inside to what my guide called the crew quarters. He opened the door to cabin #145, put down the suitcase and handed me the key, saying, "Notice that the little disk has your cabin number on it. All you have to remember is that we are on the bottom deck. Then he showed me the crew shower and said, "It's a busy place in the morning, but in the afternoon the passengers who are down here with us won't have any trouble finding an empty stall. Now I must say good night. I have to meet another passenger."

When I walked into my cabin, the first thing that hit me was the strong smell of fear. Not until I turned on the light did I see a man sitting on the bottom bunk with a haunted look on his face. I had never been this close to a starving man. His head and hands were skin and bones. I guessed he was about thirty and had seen enough terror to last him a lifetime.

I said, "I am Peter," and held out my hand. He ignored me. Resorting to sign language, I pointed at my chest and then to the upper bunk. This time he gave me a hint of a nod. As I drifted off to sleep, I wondered if a feeling of safety, plenty of food and a daily shower could bring him back to life.

Next morning I was awakened by an announcement on the public address system that breakfast would be served in the dining room daily from 8:00 a.m. until 10:00 a.m. My watch said 7:30 and my roommate was just waking up. After I finished dressing, I used gestures to show him I was going to eat and wanted him to come with me. He shook his head.

For me the first breakfast aboard was a feast of scrambled eggs, toast with marmalade and as much hot chocolate as I could hold. When I had finished eating, I asked to see the headwaiter and told him about my sick roommate.

He said, "We are not staffed for room service. I will ask the ship's doctor to have a look at him."

When I got back to our cabin, the doctor was already there. In fluent English with a slight French accent he said, "I will transfer this man to the sick bay where I can keep an eye on him. How can you stand the stench in here?" He showed me the switch to the ventilation system and turned it on. "This place will stop smelling like a pigsty by tomorrow." A few minutes later two men came in with a litter and carried the passenger away. I was relieved to be rid of the patient who was beyond caring and the doctor who didn't care.

At lunch I noticed a boy about my age sitting alone at a table for two by one of the windows. When he was there again at dinner, I went over, held out my hand and said, "Peter."

He looked up with a smile, gave me his right hand and said, "Istvan." Then he made a gesture inviting me to sit down across from him. I felt the abundance of food that suddenly surrounded us was miraculous. We ate with silent gusto since we didn't have a common language.

When we had finished stuffing ourselves, Istvan indicated to me that he wanted to show me something. Taking hold of my left elbow he guided me to a room down the hall that served as a lounge as well as a library. He walked over to a large atlas, opened it to a map and pointed to Czechoslovakia on Germany's eastern border. Then he put his index finger to his chest to indicate that was his country. I did the same for Germany. We both enjoyed our non-verbal conversation.

Next we sat down at one of the chess tables. The boards were fixed to the tabletops. Each of the pieces had a peg at its base that fit snugly into the holes in the center of the squares. In this way the game could continue even when the sea got rough.

On one of the walls of the lounge was a big map of the Atlantic Ocean. The ship's course from Europe to North America was marked by a dotted line and its position by a red pin. In the right lower corner of the map was a statement saying that the crossing normally took seven days. During the next two days Istvan and I explored the ship from bow to stern and from the engine room up to the bridge.

In the morning of the fourth day of our journey, it began to rain and walking on deck wasn't fun anymore. That afternoon the public address system suddenly came alive. "Attention all passengers and crew. This is the captain speaking. A major storm is moving towards us and will reach us this evening. Over the past twenty years the *Veendam* has repeatedly shown herself able to deal with this kind of challenge. Good seamanship requires that I head her into the storm until we move through it. Passengers and unauthorized crew will not be allowed on deck. Our arrival in New York will be delayed by two or three days. Don't worry. We are maintaining radio contact with our headquarters so that people expecting to meet passengers in New York are kept informed."

The storm struck before the dining room opened for dinner. After the captain's reassuring speech its violence surprised me. As the ship's bow alternately pointed up or down, I appreciated the handrails installed in every gangway and stairwell. When I arrived for dinner the dining room was almost empty. Istvan came shortly after I did. He had a big grin on his face, obviously enjoying the adventure.

The waiter danced over to our table and said, "You are lucky the chef and I don't get seasick, and we are lucky most passengers do. The chef is preparing a limited menu in order to keep things like soup out of people's laps. Tonight the choice is between Hungarian goulash over rice with a green salad on the side or nothing. Dessert is as much ice cream as you can eat."

I told the waiter Istvan spoke only Czech and asked him to bring my dinner so he could see it. When the goulash came, Istvan nodded enthusiastically and ordered the same. We stuffed ourselves in silence.

While the *Veendam* battled the storm, a feeling of comradeship developed among those of us who remained up and about. It must have been hard work for the crew, but for Istvan and me life became very simple: sleeping, eating, reading, and playing chess. But the magnificent power of the storm gave me a feeling of deep excitement for which I had no words. As I buckled myself into my bunk on the third night of the storm, I thought Mother *Veendam* was moving a bit more gently than the night before.

When I woke in the morning the struggle between ship and sea had definitely calmed down. That afternoon the public address system came on again. "This is the captain speaking. As you probably noticed, we have left the storm behind and are moving ahead at full speed. We will arrive in New York Harbor only three days behind schedule."

We arrived in New York on the morning of November 23, 1938. As the *Veendam* approached New York harbor shortly after dawn Istvan and I forgot about breakfast. We went on deck and watched the skyline of the city rise slowly out of the mist. All was quiet. We only heard the murmur of voices and the cries of seagulls. I had no sense that our ship was moving.

Then came a magical moment when the Statue of Liberty appeared to walk towards us out of the fog to greet us. The sobs that bubbled up from deep inside my chest surprised me. Istvan looked puzzled, but as I looked around I saw that I was not the only one who wept.

Then ordinary life announced itself when we heard the loudspeaker say: "Attention all passengers, those who are being met at the pier do not have to stop at Ellis Island. The rest must assemble on the second deck at 8 a.m. with all of their luggage, ready for transfer to the island." Istvan was one of those. Before he went below to pack his stuff, we smiled sadly at each other and shook hands and smiled again, knowing that we probably would never meet again.

NOTE: Tante Lowengard of New York City, mentioned in The Crossing, *continued to be gentle Peter's Fairy Godmother. She financed his medical school studies in New York and his internship in internal medicine at the University of Califonia's Cowell Hospital. Peter spent his entire practice in Contra Costa County, California. He retired at age seventy, much to the disappointment of his loyal patients. Peter has been widowed for some years but continues to be a devoted stepfather to his second wife's three children. The writers treasure his incisive critiques of their work and his captivating autobiography.*

STEFFI PLUMB is short and blond and energetic. She is unfailingly sweet, but when one looks closely one can notice that along with laugh lines, there is a bit of sadness. She clears her throat, takes a sip of water and a moment to look out at the class. She is, by nature, a friendly person, very upbeat and seems to have a serenity about her. She is a lover of colorful jewelry and her bracelets jangle cheerfully as if to give her courage to step back into history. Right now, the peacefulness seems to have left her and her German accent and the sadness in her eyes paint a picture even before she begins:

MEMORIES OF AN UNINVITED GUEST

Just another day in my young life, but one day I remember well. Growing up was a science. Growing up was expected of me, it was my duty. Very dutifully did I breathe in and out, held the hand of an adult on walks, visited the animals in the zoo and the reptiles in the aquarium. I ate my fruits and vegetables, played the piano and recited German poems (with distaste) to entertain whoever visited with my parents in our home.

The home often moved outwardly — the inside remained us — my parents, my sister and two sets of simply fabulous grandparents, also a nanny and Frau Kuche, the factotum, the most precious member of our family!

We moved often because my father was in the diplomatic service. I remember a time in Hangshow, another in Qazvin and another in Calcutta. I was a happy child, but never in balance with my four-year-old younger sister. I had no use for her, to the chagrin of my parents. We had just returned to Berlin from a posting. I do not remember from which country. I was so pleased to be home again. Cuddling my special pillows and my Steiff stuffed animals with a shiny smile and the next day I shall see my two cousins and visit my friends. But now I found myself on the street walking with my mother and my grandmother, returning from a visit to a relative or maybe a friend? I do not recall. But I do remember the coolness, the foggy darkness and seeing the raindrops around the lanterns, a normal late autumn day. Walking along Budapester Street, long after my bedtime and feeling especially honored and wondering why, I closely held the loving hands of the two adults and performed my *salto mortales*. Oh, what happiness! We were heading towards 'my store.' This was a very special place for me.

The long walk towards the entrance was mirrored on the ceiling and bottom and partly on the sides. I believed this must be the way to Paradise. The inside of the store was paved with mirrors also and each side displayed a beautiful car, a Maybach! Sometimes, before this night, I would stroll in wonderment to the inside to see the cars multiply in the mirrors. I always wiped little marks on the glass with the sleeve of my white coat. My store had to shine and smile at me so I could smile back.

But suddenly, a noise! It sounded like one thousand toy engines talking at the same time, piercing and sabotaging my night of wonder. I can still hear the sounds of men screaming while bombarding us with cobblestones.

Now the men in the open truck screamed with laughter at us. The rocks flew by and the sound and smell of broken glass enveloped us. I remember so well how I wanted to save my store, to stop it all. My screams into the quiet night walked us home, followed by the first sign of ugliness, the first sign of terror. We listened to the nearby ta-tu-tata of fire engines and noticed an orange-red hue in the dark sky. The next day brought us the sad news that my Aunt Lotti's so-beautiful church had burned down; the one with the cantor and a rabbi. We could not worship there anymore.

Now our home was not only filled with family. Fear had entered as an uninvited guest and the structure of our lives changed forever. Later they gave my nightmare a name. They called it *Kristallnacht*.* It was the 9th of November, 1938. I had just turned seven years old (or young).

Kristall refers to a high grade of glass often used in shop windows. This event, The Night of the Crystal, was monumental. 30,000 Jews were sent to concentration camps and released only if they obtained visas for foreign countries, after thousands of Jewish homes, shops and synagogues were smashed the length and breadth of Germany and Austria.

DRESDEN, GERMANY

FEBRUARY 13 & 14, 1945
(AGE 13)

"You wait until we arrive at home," her mother and grandmother said in stern voices. They had just left the very first meeting about air-raid etiquette. A man had been assigned to teach, among other things, how to place a gas mask with filter over a face. He, she thought, was totally inept to do so and so she felt it would be helpful if she instructed the class. After years from all the horror experienced in her hometown of Berlin, she felt qualified to demonstrate in front of about 80 people how to place the mask properly, so as to work in place. Obviously, her mother and grandmother did not agree. She knew she faced a lecture on proper respect as soon as they reached home.

Evacuated from her bombed out town, close to her beloved relatives, she now felt so secure, all of her 13 years — peace again. The sirens were ignored; day and night planes flew over on their way to Berlin, sounding heavy going and empty coming back. A forgotten bomb was dropped once or twice or three times, this on the return flight and always during day time. Nobody went to air-raid shelters because none existed. The rumor of the day said that Dresden, a beautiful, baroque city was not going to be bombed but preserved to be the new capital of Germany.

They walked home the few long blocks in the cold and very dark night. She was happy to be out at long past her bedtime, not suspecting that soon history was going to be made in a defenseless city, once known as the Florence of the North. The only lights visible were on the phosphorus buttons everybody wore so as not to walk into one another. She owned with pride several of these buttons in different styles and forms. She treasured them and treated them as pure gold. She held them up towards the sun, hopefully, to refurbish their little 'souls.' She fed them at night with artificial light and then pinned them on her garments to be ready when the sirens sounded, only to start all over with the same routine the next day. The only compromise or preparation of the city was the complete blackout of all buildings, street signs, lanterns, all transportation and private houses, all windows in houses darkened. Not one anti-aircraft battery was found in town. Military installations were 60 miles outside, because Dresden was thought to be safe from the bombing.

The sirens wailed. She walked holding on to her mother's and grandmother's hands. Suddenly the planes arrived, flying very low, fully loaded on their way to Berlin, or maybe not this time? As she looked up, the air turned gold, the stars, the buildings, the people all wrapped in gold like a beautiful present — but instead, an ugly surprise! Now they were running to their home, terrorized by noise and flashes of horror at the sudden knowledge that her life as she knew it would never be the same. More than 1,478 tons of explosives and 1,182 tons of phosphorus bombs were dropped on 1.2 million people! The city was filled with 60,000* refugees from Breslau at the eastern front. There was a hospital for wounded soldiers, thousands of them.

The firestorm finally succeeded. It had been tried before in Hamburg, Berlin, and maybe in other large cities. The perfect storm: Dresden in flames, 1600 degrees centigrade in the beautiful inner city, no survivors. She lived on the other side of the Elbe River and so her life was spared.

The fire created its own wind while it sucked the oxygen from the air. She and her family were tossed about. Sheets and curtains were ripped into strips and then tied together, people, children and animals were tied to trees or large immovable objects, always away from flames and smoke.

After a few hours they started to walk from the new town where they lived to the old city which burned for days. All their relatives lived there. More than 60,000 bodies and the remains of bodies were counted:* among them her relations, young and old, their art, their lives, works, their history. They were all too frightened to feel. The next day she and her family found themselves on the promenade near a clinic for children and pregnant women on the bank of the Elbe River. Planes arrived out of nowhere, no warning, and started shooting with their board guns at the people, one by one: nurses with babies in their arms, women about to give birth. All were running on the beautiful manicured lawns; all were killed. She and her family pressed themselves against the cold and wet grass, eyes tearing from the steady smoke, empty stomachs and painful throats, desperate without feeling, watching.

She had just played Joan of Arc in school and now was confronted with the reality of witnessing hundreds of bodies burned at the stake day and night, in a square surrounded by destroyed churches, theatres, government buildings, museums: their culture. The smell of burning flesh was sickening. The sky had disappeared and the ground looked like an island of death, of bodies, small, like burned children as the bodies shrank.

Days later back at her partly devastated home, she witnessed open wagons pulled by horses and donkeys with the monotone sound of their hooves like a funeral march. The bodies were piled high on their way to a final resting place in mass graves outside of town.

Sixty-two years later, grass has grown over the memories, over the graves, over the ruins. But those who perished in the center of the city cannot be traced. About 40,000 children, women, the elderly, wounded soldiers and the animals in the zoo were slaughtered in one night and one day.

Gerhard Hauptman had once said, "They who have lost the ability to weep learned it again at the destruction of Dresden."

*It is difficult to be accurate in the number of people massacred because of the number of wounded and refugees from many cities. Over the years very different numbers have been reported. For further information see www.DresdenGermany on the internet.

A TALE OF TWO TRAINS

ON THE OPERA TRAIN FROM BERLIN TO DRESDEN AND BACK IN 1942

O ne more week, she thought, and I will be seated on a special opera train to Dresden. Surely she would be in her red woolen dress, Russian style, white embroidered flowers with white stockings and red patent leather shoes with handbag and with a happy smile!

It was to be a big day, and the excitement mounted until it came to a crescendo the evening before. Her school work though, did not please her parents and she was not sure she would be treated to the trip. Two number 2's showed up on her report card and her parents' faces looked like a thunderstorm. However, after a short conference and her promises to do better, it was decided she could go with her parents. The train left at 18:05 sharp. The dinner was enjoyed in a beautiful compartment of the dining car with sparkling chandeliers and fresh flowers.

The music of Humperdinck's opera, *Hansel and Gretel*, sounded throughout the beauty of a building with perfect acoustics and baroque architecture which added to the warmth of the moment. We stood there so proudly. The intermission was spent indulging in sips of swallow nest soup, champagne and endless discussions about the singers, the décor, the acting and the composer. The ride home was stirring with memories of a joyful evening, never to be repeated again for her or her family, as the opera house was soon to be destroyed...

THE TRAIN TO BERLIN — MAY, 1945

To the despair of her family, the war progressed. Berlin and Dresden became cities of horror and a saga of incredible sadness began.

In May of 1945 there was surrender — a peace treaty was signed and suddenly it was all over! Her family found themselves in Dresden, a city completely in ruin; all her relatives perished in the war or in the camps. A proclamation was posted that stated that all people who migrated during the war had to return to the city they left in order to receive their ration cards. She and her father returned first. The rest of the family stayed behind to follow later. The two hours on the train to Berlin turned into a three week ordeal under terrible conditions. They found a place on the PUFFERS, the round-shaped metal disks between the train cars, the connectors. What a terrible adventure awaited them! People without resources sat or stood in their same places for weeks. The train inched along more than rolled and was slowed down by broken rails, lack of water or coal, and no food for people. At first, as a 13-year-old, she found the situation delightfully different: no school, no mother or grandmother to tell her anything. Only her dad.

Her thoughts ran wild; soon she would be home in Berlin in her own bed again. But suddenly the elements acted up. The torrential rains brought a shower without soap, at first so welcome because of the heat. But the weather changed quickly to cold and nasty winds making her shiver. The empty nights were noisy and scary, but still she felt the adventure. Slowly her pearly white skin turned darker and darker, changed by the smoke, oil and soot from the locomotive. She had no way of cleaning herself. Her teeth, the taste in her mouth and her nostrils were all dirty and greasy. But she still thought, "no destroyed structures, no airplanes dropping bombs around her, no flames blowing her around and off the ground. What is a little wind from above? She liked nature, maybe not to be outside a train car for so long, but why worry? Soon she would be back in Berlin, in her home, in her bed."

Another day and the train stopped. There was mud and devastation all around her and still half way to go! They played games to avoid hunger pangs and thirst, and the adults argued. She was allowed to sleep inside for two nights, still sitting up. But the aroma was so terrible that she was glad to be outside again.

Then came the night of blood, blood and screams that woke her up, warm blood dripping from the roof of the car onto her only outfit. What happened? The people on the top of the cars had felt safe, elevated as they said, but never realized the danger of falling off or of being decapitated by the trains going through tunnels. Body parts slid off the roofs, and when daylight appeared she saw the horror and passed out. No doctors, no nurses, no help — only prayers which helped the saved people but did nothing for the terribly wounded. Again with death around her, nature became a wasteland of sorrow, and her tears washed the last of her innocent youth away forever.

Her thoughts were again on her future, hoping against hope, that all was still there in Berlin. When they finally arrived, all was destroyed: no water, no electricity in any part of the city; only rubble to greet them. The iron gates to the subways were closed, but she could see the water logged bodies pushing to get free. The smell was so empty of anything. A faint hope marched them to the Grunewald searching for friends and relatives. The steps were so empty, but she had to be careful, always looking down, not to step on the remains of the war. Again, only silence and death as witnesses, but a faint hope propelled her into an unknown future.

NOTE: *Traumatized, her youth and most of her relatives gone, Steffi learned that no one in Germany would talk about the war after the surrender. In 1950, with a friend and borrowed money, she took off "to see the sane world." Six years later she immigrated to the U.S., leaving a German fiancé behind, met her future husband in New York City and though they moved to Montreal, they traveled every state in the union. After a divorce and relocation to San Francisco, Steffi remarried. Twenty years later her husband died suddenly. The trauma of WW II remained; she knew she "must get it out." Molly Poupeney, a beloved, now deceased member of the Rossmoor group, told her to "write it down." You've read the results. "What a catharsis it has been," says Steffi.*

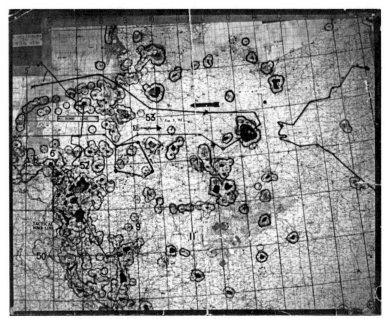

Map of Germany marked with charcoal to show flak areas and bombers flight path. "Berlin Mission, February 3, 1945. Target was airport. Heavy ground fire from gun batteries near airport. Note route flown by B-17s to avoid ground fire."

Courtesy of The National World War II Museum, New Orleans, LA

1945 — Berlin, after an Allied bombing.
**from National Archives & Records Administration (NARA),
College Park, MD.**

SUSAN HOCHSCHILD: There is nothing about Susan's serene demeanor that gives even a hint of her background. She has a British accent, and perhaps that is why one thinks of her living an orderly life, calmly dealing with whatever would come her way. She reads in the same deliberate way that she always has, but this story is that of a seven-year-old child and the memories that have been dredged up by hearing the other stories in this class.

MY MEMORIES OF VIENNA

1938—39

The storm clouds that had been gathering over Europe since 1933, as a result of Hitler's rise to power and the growth of the Nazi party, had made little impression on my serene childhood in Vienna. It was not until Hitler annexed Austria to Germany in March of 1938 when I was seven, that I slowly began to realize that the comfortable world I had known till then, was about to crumble.

I was living with my parents in a large apartment in Vienna, together with Omi, my mother's mother, my Aunt Nita who was 18 and had just graduated from high school, and my uncle Harry, who was 21 and almost finished with his Engineering Degree.

My father owned an import/export business, which required him to make frequent short business trips to nearby European countries like Poland and Czechoslovakia. I remember a lively family existence, with someone always playing the piano, frequent visitors for afternoon coffee and my mother's homemade Viennese pastries, Passover Seders around the dining room table, holidays with my parents to the Vienna Woods and other scenic spots. I also recall enjoying being the center of attention at home as the youngest, and I know I was often a pest. This was fondly mentioned by my aunt and uncle, when I tried to interrupt or join in with their games when their friends were visiting.

There are so many gaps in my recollections of those happy early days. But I do recall one particular scene: my father unexpectedly picked me up after school one day. I caught sight of him waiting outside the building, and I ran down the steps and hugged him, enjoying the familiar slight odor of his cigars.

"Daddy, you're home! I thought you were still on your trip!" I said happily.

"Well, it's your birthday! I can't be away for that, can I?" he said with a big smile as he took my hand. "I just got back this afternoon, so I thought I'd pick you up for a change. How about some ice cream at the Johann Strauss Café?" I remember how excited I was to be going out with my father for ice cream in the middle of the week. That was a rare, special treat. We walked a short distance to the café which had a view of the Danube Canal. Viennese waltzes were playing in the background, and I felt very grown up, chatting with Daddy about school and friends while enjoying my ice cream. There were mostly adults there at that time of day, businessmen reading newspapers while drinking their coffee, ladies dressed in hats and coats, talking about the opera they had seen the night before.

I realize now that most of my distinct memories are of less happy and more traumatic times. I can see Uncle Harry sitting hunched over the shortwave radio in the living room, trying to get news from other countries. I remember the eerie whistling sounds the radio made as he turned the knobs from station to station, and Omi and Mummy saying to him, with their hands over their ears, "Please, Harry, not so loud! We get enough bad news in the local paper…" Occasionally we would hear a loud grating voice declaiming at great length. I soon learned that it was the voice of Hitler, as he ranted hysterically, spreading his poison from city to city around Germany.

There were other scenes that stand out in my mind as foreshadowing the turmoil that was about to break out in Austria in the spring of 1938, probably shortly after the annexation of Austria to Germany. My mother and I were walking down a street on a shopping trip in our neighborhood where we'd walked many times before, but that day everything looked and sounded different. As we turned a familiar corner, we saw huge banners in red, white and black, each with a swastika emblazoned in the middle, hanging from many buildings; officers in uniforms were everywhere, and they looked threatening as they moved around the crowded pavement, shouting over loudspeakers. Some people were just standing, their right hands raised and staring ahead, others were quickly moving away from the commotion.

"Mummy, what are all those flags?" I remember asking. "Why do some of those people around the building have their hands up, and why are they saying, 'Hi, Hitler?'"

"Well, Susie, Austria has become part of Germany now, and that's the German flag, and those officers and people are just saluting it," my mother said with a frown and quickly changed the subject. Somehow I wasn't reassured; I didn't understand. I know that at that time I had no idea what the swastika represented, but my mother obviously did, and she held my hand more tightly as we returned home instead of doing the shopping we had planned. Even now, so many years later, whenever I see a swastika banner, in movies or on television, hanging from a building, the same feelings of fear and revulsion come over me.

At that time my father was on one of his business trips to Poland. I know now that there were many phone conversations between my mother and him. One time I overheard them talking, and I wanted to get on the phone and talk to Daddy myself, until I heard her saying:

"Please, Robert, don't try to come back yet! You know how much we want to see you, but so many men have been arrested — Joe Kopperman and Fred Feinberg. It's not good here right now! …No, we're safe here at the moment, but…" She saw me standing there, and waved me away, saying, "Tomorrow you can talk to Daddy. Not now."

Poland at that time was still considered safer than Vienna, but that safety didn't last long. I recently came across a family file with some old letters from my father, which made it clear that he was working with the consulate in Warsaw trying to get a visa to go to the U.S. or to England in the hope that we could join him there, and he sounded confident that this would happen soon. When I see these letters now in that familiar handwriting, sounding so sure that we would all be together soon, I become quite emotional. Maybe he was trying to reassure himself as well as my mother.

It seemed the phone was in constant use that summer. Many friends were calling; some had been able to arrange for visas to countries where they had relatives, like the U.S., England, or South America. Others called with sad stories of sudden family losses. I remember asking what was happening, but I was always diverted and told not to worry. I'm sure I did worry deep down, but I was only seven, and, on the surface, my life hadn't changed too much yet, though I desperately missed my father.

One day in June of 1938, my uncle came home from the university out of breath and shaking. For a change, I was right there when he came home and heard the whole unedited story.

"I'd just left the campus area and was walking over to the bus stop," he began, still out of breath, "and I heard voices yelling out to me, 'Hey, Jew-boy, come over here!' I turned around and saw that it was that Hans Mueller who was in my class in high school. He's now in the Hitler Youth, and he was with some Gestapo officers across the street— and they were all yelling at me to stop— I didn't even think of stopping, I just ran around the corner as fast as I could— I was so scared, Mutti! When I got to that big lamp store, I took off my school jacket, bunched it up in front of me, and bent over to look at a lamp in the store window!" He took another deep breath, and continued, "Somehow they all ran past cursing, and they didn't notice me!"

"Ah, thank God!" my grandmother cried out, her hands to her tear-stained face. She hugged him tightly. Then we all hugged him afterwards, one by one, as if our hugs might keep him safe the next time. I noticed he was still perspiring heavily when he finally sat down in the living room.

So when Uncle Harry told the family a few days later that he wanted to apply for a visa to Italy, where a friend of his from the university had relatives and where they would be able to find work as engineers, my mother and grandmother and I just hugged and kissed him tearfully and wished him well. It wasn't long before he took off. As it happened, Italy turned out not to be such a safe haven after all because Hitler had kept on marching across Europe, and soon Uncle Harry was on the move again. After many adventures, sometimes traveling with fake papers, he finally arrived and settled in America in 1941 and it was through him that I, many years later, was able to come here.

As I try to recall what happened next, it feels as if I'm recalling memories of memories, rather than the events themselves. There was one afternoon that I remember going to the public library with my mother and aunt, and they suggested that I browse through the children's department while they looked up some reference materials. I looked at several books, and then wandered over to the Reference Department where I saw them both paging through several big heavy looking phone books. I know they told me then that there were looking for people in the U.S. and England with Jewish names to contact, to see if they could possibly sponsor us and help with getting visas for our family. I know I foolishly whined, "But I don't want to go to another country. I just want Daddy to come home again and be with us all!" I let them reassure me somehow, but I knew they were both writing down names, addresses and phone numbers.

That fall some of our friends managed to leave Vienna

for other countries. Many of them had lost their jobs or businesses and some men had been deported. My father's attempts in Poland to obtain a visa for the U.S. failed due to a bureaucratic error even though he had somehow been able to find a sponsor there. His first name on the visa was wrong, even though all the other facts, like date of birth and address were correct, and the whole procedure had to be started all over again, by which time it was too late for him to be allowed to leave Poland, where anti-Semitism had become rampant, and sadly, though we continued to hear from him from time to time, eventually only through brief heavily censored letters through the Red Cross, we never saw him again.

One bit of good news was that searching the international phone books had helped my aunt Nita find a sponsor. By making many phone calls to Jewish agencies in London, my mother located a family in Manchester in the North of England, that was willing not only to bring Aunt Nita over, but ultimately to help the rest of us get settled there also. My aunt was hired by this family as a domestic helper for their large family, and she left for England in October. From her phone calls and letters we learned that the Segal family was treating her very well. "Yes, Mutti, I'm working hard. My English is so much better... all the family are very kind to me, and I can't wait till you're all here with me. Mr. Segal showed me some small houses that we could rent when you all get here..." Omi relayed this conversation to us after one of my aunt's phone calls.

I do remember that I was very unhappy and worried about the prospect of leaving our home and life in Vienna, but clearly our old life was gone. There was no music or laughter or playtime any more, just serious discussion. Sometimes, if

I wandered into a room, my mother would start speaking to my grandmother in Polish, which I knew wasn't a good sign.

I could sense an increase in anxiety around the apartment during the next few weeks. My mother seemed to be very preoccupied with the telephone and packing things in small boxes, papers in large folders, and with listening intently to news broadcasts. One day in November, I remember coming home early from school, and found my mother standing on a chair in one of the bedrooms, in front of a very tall chest of drawers, putting what looked like a large envelope into the top drawer. I stood in the doorway, about to greet her, and then instinctively backed out. Somehow I felt I wasn't supposed to see what she was doing. I softly walked out into the hall, greeted my grandmother who gave me the usual warm hug; she had no idea that I hadn't just come in at the front door. Later as we ate dinner, they talked about something that happened the previous day in Germany, something serious, and they seemed very worried that there would now be more problems for Jews. Even though they were speaking German, I just couldn't understand what had happened the previous day, November 9, 1938. I know now that some major anti-Jewish violence had erupted throughout Germany on that day.

Some time after dinner our doorbell rang insistently, with the two short and two long beeps that our family had begun to use. My mother and grandmother looked at each other and at me, but then opened the door hesitantly. Two heavyset Gestapo officers pushed their way in, each carrying a large package and began barking out orders. I was trembling with fear as they tramped through the hallway, "Where is Robert

Klinger?" (my father), they demanded. When my mother told them he was on a business trip, they continued searching through all the rooms, even looking on the balcony. The three of us followed along behind them.

Then the older of the two said in a harsh voice, "Where is all your silver?" My mother mutely opened cabinets and drawers in the living room and dining room, and then they opened up the packages they were carrying and took out several heavy black carrying bags, in which they tossed the silverware, and other antique objects that caught their eyes, yelling for napkins and towels to wrap some of them up. They took oil paintings off the wall, and stacked them near the front door. Then the senior of the two told the other one to stay near the door with the silver and paintings and said he wanted to go through the apartment again. So he tramped through all the rooms again, opening more cabinets, taking books off shelves and looking behind them, throwing the books on the floor as he worked his way through. Finally he arrived back at the bedroom where I had seen my mother hiding the large envelope earlier that day. He looked under the beds, and then I held my breath as he worked his way around the room. I couldn't take my eyes off that tall cabinet as he opened the top drawer, looked inside, threw various objects on the floor, and continued with the other drawers, all of which he left open. But he hadn't found that envelope! (Much later I found out that what my mother had put away was money she had taken out of the bank that morning and that there was a hidden button in the back of that top drawer, which revealed a deeper drawer beneath it.) Then the officer tramped back through all the rooms to the front door where the other officer was waiting. I was beginning to feel relief as they finally seemed to be ready to go, but then he looked back at my mother and barked, "You come with us and carry the bags with the silver!" My mother looked terrified as did my grandmother, and I began to cry, but my mother kissed us both, and then walked out slowly and slightly bent over, carrying those heavy bags filled with silver, wedged between the two tall officers who casually carried the paintings under their arms. As my grandmother closed the door, I saw she was quietly sobbing too, and we held each other tightly. I think we were both afraid to express the terror that we felt that we might never see my mother again. But about two hours later she returned, white, shaken and disheveled with a huge red bruise on her cheek. She told us tearfully that when they arrived at headquarters with all our possessions, she had asked if she could have a receipt, and that one of the Gestapo officers took great pleasure in slapping her in the face and pushing her out the door!

I don't think any of us got much sleep that night. Aside from the traumatic events of the day for us, there was lots of noise outside, voices shouting, a strong smell of burning. What we found out the next morning was that throughout Austria and Germany the Nazis had burned and destroyed over 250 synagogues, killed more than 100 people, smashed any Jewish stores that still existed, and had begun the incarceration of thousands into concentration camps. This orchestrated event is now known as *Kristallnacht* (The Night of the Broken Glass), and caused almost everyone who could, to leave as quickly as possible for safer places. Unfortunately, very few countries were willing to take in Jewish refugees even after this event, and the conditions for admittance were very strict.

I didn't go to school the next morning, but the following day I did go back. Our always harsh principal called the whole school together in an assembly and announced that beginning the following week, Jewish children would have to go to a different school, because they no longer belonged at the school we'd been attending. None of us seven-year-olds understood quite what was going on, or why this was happening, but I distinctly remember how humiliated we felt, especially when some of our former friends would barely speak to us at recess.

Going to the new school the following week was actually better than expected. I realized much later how hard many people must have worked to find another location for a school, but somehow they did. Although it was farther from home and the classes much more crowded than before, I already knew many of the children and a couple of Jewish teachers from my old school who had lost their jobs there. I think I got my first introduction to learning English in that school, to prepare us for our eventual emigration. A great deal of emphasis was placed on conversation and vocabulary, and I enjoyed learning something completely different. I would come home and try to talk to my mother in English whenever she spoke to my grandmother in Polish just to show I too could speak another language!

The atmosphere at home was tense and frightening. My mother spent hours on the phone and listened constantly to radio news, which was never good, much of it telling of the advance of Hitler's troops. I remember the day she sat down with me in the living room, her arms around me and told me in a gentle voice that she had managed to get a place for me on a ship that would take me to England where I would stay with the Segal family with Aunt Nita until she and Omi could join me. This ship would have mostly children and some adults, and several such ships had already arrived safely. I remember bursting into tears as soon as she started telling me this— I had been doing a bit of eavesdropping the last few weeks and had suspected something. I knew some of my friends at school had mysteriously stopped coming to school, and I was afraid. But my mother reassured me about her plans and said she and my grandmother already had applied for visas and would follow me to England shortly.

"And what about Daddy?" I remember asking.

"He's doing everything he can, darling, working with the consulate, and we're sure he'll soon be joining us in England," she answered, stroking my hair, and I let myself be reassured.

So it was arranged for me to leave Vienna on March 13, 1939 by train to join one of the Kindertransport voyages to England. The British government had decided to admit an unspecified number of children up to age 17 to England if foster families could be found. In my case, the Segal family had agreed to sponsor me and the rest of the family.

I remember almost nothing of that journey to England. I know we arrived at the main train station in Vienna in the early evening, the platform full of crying children of all ages, with tearful parents giving last-minute kisses and instructions. We registered with a woman at a table and a big name tag was put on my coat and suddenly there was a flurry of announcements, and it was time to say our final good-byes and get on the train. We were all in tears, children and adults alike, and as the train pulled slowly away, we children all waved vigorously as our families grew smaller and smaller.

I was in a compartment with several young girls and boys and a couple of teenagers. The train had stopped at the far end of the station, when the door opened and a Gestapo officer burst in, demanding to see everyone's papers. I was sitting on the lap of a teenage girl at the time, and I remember how she began to tremble when the officer came in, and of course, I trembled on her lap too. We all dug into our belongings and handed our papers to him one at a time. He looked at each one carefully, then handed them back without a word, and left the compartment. Someone from the window seat called out, "He just got off!" The train began to speed up, and we all relaxed a little, and started to talk. I think many of us dozed or slept from sheer nerves and exhaustion. At some point much later, we heard one of the teenage boys call out, "There's a windmill, we must be in Holland!" Soon the train ground to a halt, the doors opened, and several women came on to the train, welcomed us in German and told us to take all our belongings, and that food was waiting. We were ushered to a large area, where huge tables were set up with all kinds of sandwiches, cheese, cake, cookies and lemonade, and I think by then we were all pretty hungry. We were welcomed again by several people and were told that shortly we would be taken to the ship moored nearby that would take us to England. We were at The Hague, in Holland, close to the North Sea!

The sea voyage is another blank in my memory. I know it was an overnight trip and that we landed in Harwich, England in the morning of March 15, 1939. Here, too, we were led to another large indoor area, again with laden tables of sandwiches and cake, with many people standing, waving and waiting for us. I felt excited to hear some English being spoken and to actually understand what was being said to us. Someone called out names and children came forward shyly and were led to whoever was waiting for them. I looked nervously around while I waited. When my turn finally came, a young man came forward, holding a photograph of me standing in front of our apartment building in Vienna! He was Mark Segal, one of the Segal family's sons, he told me. With a smile he said he was bringing me love from Aunt Nita, and said he would drive me to Manchester to the family home. I felt so relieved. He picked up my suitcase as I waved goodbye to some of my shipmates who were still waiting to be met, and I walked hand in hand with Mark Segal into my new life in a new country.

I remember very little of the car trip up to Manchester. I know I felt nervous about what was ahead of me, and also carsick, since I had rarely been in a car before and only on short trips. Also my English was too limited for much conversation, and his German was even more limited, and I gave in to the overwhelming urge to sleep, and dozed on and off for most of the three-hour trip, waking up now and then to hear the radio playing softly, and English being spoken.

I have one brief but vivid memory of our arrival at the Segal house. As we pulled up in front, and got out of the car, it began to drizzle lightly under a grey and leaden sky — which I learned later, was typical Manchester weather. I looked in amazement at the large house, and at the huge expanse of garden with flowering bushes in front. I wasn't used to anything like that in Vienna, where we had lived in the city, and where everyone we knew lived in apartments. Later on I realized that the house and garden weren't really as large as they seemed to me that momentous first day.

As I looked out, the front door opened, and I saw my aunt Nita running out, followed more slowly by other members of the family. It was wonderful to be hugged and kissed by her, my dear and familiar auntie whom I hadn't seen for six months. We all went into the house, and gradually I was introduced to the rest of the family, Mr. and Mrs. Segal, and their two teenage daughters. They were all warm and welcoming and seemed as curious about me as I was about them. I remember how inadequate I felt with my halting English as they asked me questions about the journey and about my family.

The table in the dining room was all set for afternoon tea, with cucumber sandwiches, crumpets and small cakes on three-tiered serving dishes. As we sat down, there was lots of conversation and laughter around the table, and suddenly I found myself saying to the family what I had practiced so hard the last few days, "Senk you verry much to let me come to England!" Aunt Nita gave me a big hug and a proud smile, and Mr. and Mrs. Segal said, "Isn't she sweet?" as they patted my arm. I could feel tears coming again, and tried to sniff them away. So much had happened in the last few days, and I felt completely overwhelmed. Somehow I knew that my life was never going to be the same again, and yet I felt hopeful about the future.

NOTE: Susan's mother and grandmother joined her a month later. She remained in England until after her college graduation. In 1953, she immigrated to Philadelphia where her Uncle Harry — from her story — had settled. She married, earned a Masters Degree in Library Science, and worked as a suburban Library Director for many years, then moved west to join her family. "Mingling with so many talented people (in the Writers Group) has become an important part of my life," she states. It was particularly painful and difficult for Susan to revisit her early childhood — yet cleansing. Another bonus: three grateful children who had always heard her gloss over that era, until Memories of Vienna.

Translated caption for these two photos reads, "Germany, 10 November, 1938. Display windows in fragments after the Kristallnacht."

**Photos from the government website of the
Emilia-Romagna Region in Italy**

 *OTTO SCHNEPP is fairly new to the class. He joined with the idea of doing some autobiographical writing, and so the idea of* Designated Heroes *was an excellent beginning. His demeanor as he reads the reactions of that 13-year-old boy forced to leave all that he had known to flee the Nazis, remains calm and steady. As others have done when first sharing these experiences, he occasionally pauses to take a deep breath before continuing.*

UNDER NAZI RULE
FIVE VIGNETTES

INTRODUCTION

The events I describe here are my own experiences, as I remember them. I believe the account is quite accurate except for some details of the dialogue. The events all took place in Vienna after the annexation of Austria by Germany in March, 1938 and before my immigration to Shanghai in late January, 1939. Shanghai was chosen as refuge by approximately 20,000 Jews from Germany, Austria and Poland, because it was at that time the only place in the world where people without means could immigrate without the requirement of a visa. This was so because Shanghai was, in part, an international city and not part of any country.

In view of the fact that Germany invaded Poland, triggering the outbreak of WWII on September 1st 1939, it may seem that my parents and I left Nazi Germany in the nick of time. Yet it all happened within less than one year. There just was not much time to make decisions to uproot lives, raise the means necessary for fares — the voyage to Shanghai took four weeks and was commensurately expensive — and to complete all necessary formalities. And this is not to speak of the courage and determination it took to go to foreign and distant shores facing a future devoid of certainty. I turned 13 in July 1938 and did not confront the question of survival, but my parents certainly must have faced that question. It is to my father's credit that he pushed for our leaving with great energy, and he had the foresight to understand that the danger to our survival was even greater to remain where we were. As it turned out, my father's judgment proved accurate, and I am indebted to his wisdom for my survival.

The shrill ring of the door bell cut through the calm of the apartment, followed by several more jarring bursts. The maid opened the front door, and three men in civilian clothes burst in unceremoniously.

One of them called out in a loud voice, "Is the man at home?"

The maid replied, "No, he is not at home. Only the mistress is here." Her voice had a slight quiver and signaled uncertainty and discomfort — perhaps even some fear.

"Where is he?" the intruder shot back.

"Probably at his job," was the response. Her voice had steadied and conveyed a trace of resistance.

I was in that apartment visiting a school friend, as I had often done before. We were 12 years old, going on 13. I was aware that these people must be Nazi officials, probably of the feared GESTAPO.

They took charge of the apartment, and one of them said to the maid in Viennese dialect and in a commanding tone, "You and I will wait downstairs in the car for the man of the house to return. You will point him out to me when he comes."

The maid made no response. She seemed to have decided to bow to the Nazi's order. The other two strangers took command of the premises. The parents of my friend were Jewish while the maid obviously was not. I was in a state of shock and did not know what to do. I was uncertain if I could sit down but was afraid to ask. Play was out of the question. Both of us boys stood around as if paralyzed, barely making any move and instinctively avoided attracting attention. None of us spoke. My friend's mother was somewhere, but she showed no sign of her presence. I imagined that she was in a back room being questioned, but I heard only some murmurs.

My mind was racing, posing questions to which I had no answers. What was happening? What would become of me? Would they take me away, as I knew they had taken many Jewish men in those days of spring 1938, following the *Anschluss* (annexation) of Austria to Nazi Germany. True, in all instances I had heard of, the men were grown-ups. But who knew? I had witnessed the Viennese welcoming the German troops with enthusiasm in March, 1938, and later when Hitler visited, he was greeted as a liberator. Jews, by edict and by the evidence of cruel and suppressive actions, had been declared an underclass without rights and were now free game, exposed to random and capricious physical attacks. Bands of teenagers could and did attack young boys like me. I had begun to admit to myself that nobody, including my parents, had the power to protect me.

My parents had always thought of themselves as Austrian, and this conviction was a basic part of their personalities. My father had fought in the Austrian army for all four years of WWI and had earned three military decorations with crossed swords on their ribbons indicating that they had been awarded "for actions of bravery in the face of the enemy." All this past had now been denied and invalidated.

As a child, I had not been taught any of the values of Jewish culture and therefore had no defenses against the Nazis' slanderous distortions of the Jewish personality and character. I was vulnerable and open to absorbing the anti-Semitic propaganda freely dispersed by Göebbels, Hitler's propaganda minister, and his publication *Der Stürmer*. I felt rudderless, unworthy and confused as now, in retrospect, I believe my parents were as well. We all lived in a state of bewilderment and fear. My father seemed to me to be the only one who retained an outside calm and never let on that there was an impending threat hanging over us. This image of steadiness was a source of comfort to me and, I believe, to my mother and my sister as well.

The telephone rang several times, and one of the Nazis answered it, "The telephone is closed."

An hour, perhaps more, must have passed in this state of suspense and fear. Then the doorbell rang again— this time just a single burst followed by silence. One of the men opened the door, and there stood my 15-year-old sister.

"What do you want?" I heard the man ask.

I was surprised and encouraged by her firm reply, "I have

come to take my brother home!"

"Where is he?"

"There," she responded pointing at me. The Nazi was obviously nonplussed.

"Take him away then," I heard him say.

I felt a surge of relief and joy, took my jacket and we marched out. My sister was my heroine of the day! She had come, braved the dragon and had rescued me. I felt reassured by the knowledge that there was somebody else besides my father in the family who kept a sense of coolness and dignity.

UNDER ATTACK

"Here we say HEIL HITLER," a youngster's voice rang out, directed at me after I had entered the stationery store and had called out a conventional greeting, "*Gross Gott.*"

I knew that I had been marked as a Jew and stiffened with fear of the consequences. I nevertheless proceeded purposefully with the intended purchase and left the store. I was frightened. I was aware that several youngsters, perhaps a year or two older than I, had left the store and were waiting outside. There were no viable options. I could not escape them by running, I knew. There was nobody in the store or outside who would help me. I was alone and expecting to be attacked and beaten up, at the least. I contracted my chest as if to armor myself against the impending danger and began to walk in the direction of my grandmother's house, where my parents and I had moved after giving up our apartment.

The move was necessary after my father, a physician, was not allowed to practice any more. As a Jew, he was not allowed to treat non-Jews. Fortunately, the apartment was quite roomy, although it was even by the standards of Vienna of those days, old-fashioned and limited; the toilet had to be flushed with a bucket, and the furniture clearly was dated to the turn of the century. My sister had left in August for Kenya in East Africa, then a British Crown Colony, where a brother of my father's lived. She had just had her 16th birthday.

A group of four or five boys followed me. They called out, in turn: "Dirty Jew, coward, stop and fight! We ought to kill all of you Jews!"

But they still refrained from attacking me and contented themselves with jostling me now and again. I just kept on walking, my movements had become automatic, and I did not allow myself to be aware of my feelings. All my senses were concentrated on survival. I was on the lookout for escape routes or opportunities, but none presented themselves. It became clear to me that the boys were undecided as to what to do, and I pinned my hopes on that conclusion.

After about ten minutes of this impasse, we arrived at the house. I stopped in front of the entrance to the building without knowing why I did not run in to escape. Perhaps I did not want them to intrude on the house itself. Or I sensed that I might be at greater risk if I ran, and they went after me and caught hold of me.

One of them soon spoke up, "Why did you stop?"

"I live here," I responded.

Two of them then attacked me and I took a number of blows to my body and one landed on my face in the area of my right eye. I did not try to defend myself. With that they turned and left. I ran into the house unimpeded. I shook, as my body relaxed and allowed my feelings to surface. After a few minutes, I was calmer and went upstairs.

My grandmother opened the door. She did not seem to notice anything out of the ordinary. Soon I felt some pain and realized that I had a very black eye. I eventually regained my composure and actually felt victorious and congratulated myself on having gotten away with minor damage, although the black eye was an obvious reminder for many days.

My grandmother was the first to notice the bruises on my face and exclaimed, "What happened to you?"

I explained that I had been called names and been beaten up some, but I hurried to add that I was alright, and it would all pass quickly. My mother was also worried and sympathetic, but my father avoided asking me for details. I got the message that it was best to make light of the experience.

A few days later my Uncle Gyuri visited, and he inquired of my parents with obvious concern, "What happened to Burschi?" using the endearment my late grandfather had used for me.

My father quickly responded, "Just a fight among boys!"

My uncle replied, "Ah so," and that was it. I said nothing, and the uncle did not inquire further.

I understand now that this was a significant experience, and I still carry in me some remnants of sadness and fear, as I relive it while writing. I had now learned for sure that I was physically unsafe, and nobody could protect me. I have since concluded that my father's feelings of impotence probably caused him to prefer denial to facing up to the reality that all of us were not safe, although he was the most threatened.

KRISTALLNACHT

It was close to noon on November 10, 1938. There was a knock on the outside door. My grandmother opened it and in burst my Aunt Mitzi, my father's younger sister.

"Get Bruno quickly away from here," she almost shouted with a nervous energy which even for her was at an unusual level. She referred to my father who had been living under self-imposed house arrest since our move to avoid attracting any attention in this neighborhood where he was not known.

Mitzi continued in staccato telegraphic style, "They are arresting Jews all over the city. They have burned synagogues. They have broken into all Jewish stores and have emptied them. I took Gustl and Gert (her husband and son) to a Christian friend, and they are hiding out there. I rushed over to warn you in the hope that you are still unharmed. You must take Bruno to a safe place. Perhaps the Malinkonis. But hurry, by all means hurry."

My parents conferred briefly and decided to take a taxi and to go to the Malinkonis' house, where the wife was an old friend of Mother's. Both she and her husband were Italian citizens and the husband was Catholic.

My father spoke up, "We will go, and you will stay here."

I felt my heart sink, and terror gripped me. I loved my grandmother and trusted her to do what she could for me, but at 13, I was fully conscious of the cloud of danger and fear which had invaded the room, and I did not want to be separated from my parents. With a sob accompanying my words I burst out, "No, I want to come along with you. I do not want to stay!" Unhesitatingly, my father agreed and we left my grandmother's apartment on foot to go to the taxi stand a few blocks away.

As the taxi turned the corner, I had full view of a Jewish jewelers' shop by the name of Scheer. A large crowd stood outside the broken show window with several SS Nazi storm troopers in uniform among them. No police were in evidence. On some of the surviving show windows there were still fragments of the repeated painted inscriptions identifying the store as a Jewish business. The store seemed in disarray and empty of merchandise. The image, nearly 70 years old, is clearly imprinted on my memory, and I still feel remnants of the terror which it conveyed at the time.

Miraculously, as I understood later, we arrived at the Malinkonis' without incident and the lady of the house was at home. There was no telephone at my grandmother's house and therefore my parents had no means of communicating and warning Mrs. Malinkoni of our impending arrival, and therefore the lady's presence at her home was a great relief for us. We had arrived at a 'safe house.' The risk of her not being at home was never discussed during the taxi ride — the ever-present fear of possible events of unknown nature must have been on my parents' mind. I, myself, was too fearful to even think at all coherently.

Later, Mr. Malinkoni himself arrived and greeted my parents, welcoming them and assuring them of his efforts to protect my father.

He added, however, "I have heard a great deal of what is happening around the city and the country from Italian embassy sources. I will not allow you, Bruno, to leave my house today. It is too dangerous. You must spend the night here. I believe that it is safe for Erzsi and the boy to go home.

I must tell you that I am really glad that you succeeded getting here, because I have heard of taxis being stopped and Jewish men being dragged out and arrested. What will happen to those taken into custody we don't know at this time."

The threat implied in this last pronouncement hung in the air. By then the existence of concentration camps and the harsh treatment prisoners experienced there were common knowledge. The word *Dachau* sent shivers down my spine. I had also heard rumors of remains of detainees having been returned to families in sealed coffins, meaning that they were to be interred without being opened.

This was my exposure to the events of the infamous *Kristallnacht*. My father returned home safely two days later, and our lives continued, but the threat of harm and constant danger in alien surroundings had been ratcheted up significantly. It had become clear that Jews had to try to leave to save themselves. My parents looked for opportunities with renewed vigor and settled on plans to leave for Shanghai in late January 1939.

ABANDONED

It was a day in late November 1938. As I entered the apartment I faced an unexpected scene. Two suitcases were lying open on top of the bed visible through the open door. My parents were there, packing clothes, and my grandmother hovered aimlessly in the front room, obviously in a state of agitation. I had returned from a visit to a friend who lived close by, expecting a calm family scene with preparations for dinner in progress. The scene I faced did not fit. What was going on?

My father interrupted his activity and came over to where I stood. I was in a state of surprise, bordering on shock, and full of foreboding and fear of the unknown.

He addressed me in a tremulous voice with moist eyes, not at all in character. "We had the unexpected opportunity to exchange tickets for Shanghai with a couple who could not leave because their papers were not ready. The man had been incarcerated, and it will take a few weeks to assemble the required documents for their leaving. We wanted you to leave with me and leave Mutti (mummy) behind, but our arrangements don't allow that. As you know, we have our booking for January with you and Mutti traveling in a women's cabin, and you cannot go in a women's cabin without being accompanied by your mother or another woman. Gyuri pushed for us to take advantage of this opportunity for me to get out of the country and to safety. But this means that you have to stay with Oma and follow with this couple in January. We know that this will be hard on you. We don't see any other way out... ."

His voice faded out. He was actually crying now. I had never seen my father cry! His armor had cracked. He did not comfort me. I now believe that he was too conflicted about the decision to leave me behind and was afraid of losing control even further. My mother hovered in the background and also did not come forward with words or gestures of comfort. I was alone.

I stood there as if thunderstruck. My legs felt weak. I was scared. I cried openly in spite of trying hard to hold back the tears. The logic was indisputable. My father was the one in the greatest danger. But my innards were in turmoil. And my tears flowed uncontrollably. For the next hour I just stood around, forlorn and waiting for the inevitable to happen. My subdued crying continued.

My father tried to comfort my mother. "He cannot help crying," he said several times. This was true, but it did not give me any comfort. The time came, and we all went to the train station by taxi. There I met the couple I would travel with. Tearfully, I parted from my parents, and at this point, they both hugged me with sadness in their eyes, and their embrace gave expression to their love and, I imagine, their feelings of guilt.

The train started up, and they were gone. In spite of all the logic, I felt alone and abandoned. Over half a century later, I still cannot recall the event without my eyes filling with tears.

All I had left was the hope that I would be able to follow my parents to Shanghai without any further problems. However, there was no certainty in which I could seek comfort.

THE PASSPORT

One day in early January 1939, I woke up in the morning and then sat up like a shot. The realization struck me like a thunderbolt: I did not have a passport! And I was scheduled to leave Vienna at the end of January to rejoin my parents in Shanghai!

What to do? When my parents left, my father had asked me to try to secure an export permit for an electric instrument used to remove warts and the like. After some hesitation, I had gone to the appropriate government agency to make the required application. This in itself was no small matter. The Nazi authorities seemed threatening to me after all that I had seen and heard, and I felt at risk going to an office where I had to face what seemed to me to be a superior being invested with absolute power over me. This was, of course, also valid for any grown-up Jew and all the more for me, a mere child of 13. However, to my relief, things went smoothly, but I had to leave my passport with the application. At the time I thought nothing of it, assuming that the permit would be granted quickly. But now, several weeks had passed, and I was seized by panic at the thought that I might not be able to leave as scheduled. My fate really depended on getting back that passport.

I decided to take a decisive step and go once more to the same office and ask for my passport, even if it meant withdrawing the application. Again, I was intimidated by the thought of facing another official, but this time there was a lot at stake. I had no choice but to pump up my courage again and go into the lion's den.

I walked through the streets feeling much anxiety. I had come to know that my fear of danger was lodged in the small of my back. It was as if I expected somebody to stick a knife in there as I went by. I passed a number of Nazi storm troopers in their brown uniforms with swastika armbands, and every time I had this sensation.

I stood in line, the only youngster of my age in the company of mostly women, because men were considered more at risk of arbitrary arrest. We had plenty of time to converse, and many were interested to know how a young boy came to be there. I told my story several times and got advice on how to handle the feared confrontation. Several thought I should cry to get sympathy. I rejected that. I needed to be strong, and again I armored myself by contracting my chest.

Finally, the moment came. I presented my case for emigration and requested to get my passport back. At that point, I felt myself trembling, waiting for the verdict. The official in front of me seemed a decent person. I even was tempted to see him as sympathetic although his face remained expressionless. He got up without uttering a word, left his post and disappeared behind a wall. I stood there, in a state of suspense and trembling slightly but still outwardly controlled.

The official reappeared with a file in his hand. His face still did not convey any message. I strained and saw my name on the file. He put it down, opened it, and there was my passport. My heart missed a beat. Without uttering a word, he took the passport and handed it to me!

The danger was over, and I walked out and back home feeling triumphant. I had secured my passport in my pocket, concealed from sight. It felt safer that way. I told my grandmother about my success, and she was pleased. She assured me that she had put her trust in me and had expected me to measure up to the task. Her reaction felt good, but I also was a bit disappointed. I would have liked her to make more of a fuss. She did not seem to appreciate the trauma I had experienced, nor the enormity of the challenge I had faced.

I did leave Vienna on time and rejoined my parents in Shanghai where we faced new difficulties in an alien environment.

My grandmother never made it out. She was murdered at Terecin (Theresienstadt).

NOTE: Otto and his family remained in Shanghai until at age twenty-two he earned a B.S. degree. He received a Ph.D. in chemistry from the University of California at Berkeley, taught for thirteen years at the Israel Institute of Technology and at the University of Southern California until retirement in 1992. In 'retirement' he directed the East Asian Studies Center at the University of Southern California for six years. His wife Eileen (see Little David*) urged him to join the class where he has found it useful to recall and reflect on his life experiences through writing and to value the input of its members and facilitator, Mary Webb.*

FRANK WEINMAN has a very European air about him and a wry sense of humor. He is fond of quoting historical tidbits and can poke gentle fun. There is nearly always a twinkle in his eye but not today. He begins by apologizing for his accent (which is actually quite charming) and then tells his stories.

GENTLE HANDS

We were a closely knit family, but we were not important people, with one exception: Professor Josef Novak. He was a first cousin of my mother, a gynecologist who delivered both my older brother and me. My mother swore by him, and she was quite sure that he was the best gynecologist in all of Vienna. "He has such gentle hands," she often said.

Actually, it was not only his wonderful way of treating patients, but also the fact that he had written a book which had been translated into many languages, English among them. Many American patients came to Vienna just to see Professor Josef Novak. This meant that his practice was quite lucrative. He lived and had his practice close to the University of Vienna.

When Josef Novak was 40 years old, he decided that it was time for him to get married and have children. However, he did not want a Jewish wife. He knew about the recessive genes and the high incidence of Tay-Sachs Disease in Jews. He was concerned that if he had the recessive gene and married a woman with the same gene, their children could suffer from the disease. It is for that reason, I believe, that he refused all the matches my mother and other well meaning relatives suggested. No, he wanted a gentile woman!

Actually, such a woman was not hard for him to find. His own nurse, who of course had to be present when he examined a woman patient, would fit the requirement. Her name was Hertha Oberdorf. She came from the Austrian provinces, was rather pretty without being beautiful, and most likely in love with her boss because when he suggested marriage she immediately accepted.

Sure enough within a few years Hertha bore three girls. All was going well for the Novaks when Hitler and his Nazi hordes came to Austria in 1938.

Dr. Novak recognized that he was in danger. To protect his family, he divorced his wife, relinquishing all his possessions to her. He didn't want her to have the burden of being married to a Jew. Actually, such divorces were not uncommon in Vienna at that time because the non-Jews and their children would be considered Jewish and shipped to concentration camps to be executed.

Josef Novak immediately applied for and obtained permission to leave the Third Reich. "Just get out," they said. "We do not need any Jewish doctors in Germany." Thanks to his reputation in England, he immediately found employment there.

Hertha had plans of her own. She went to the Gestapo, the dreaded secret police, and stated her case. "I am an Aryan woman and had to live with this ugly Jew for many years. You will forgive me if I tell you that I have my love life with other men, all good Aryans. The children were not the Jew's." Thus Hertha achieved her goal. She was an Aryan, her children were declared Aryans, and she now had no problems taking everything Professor Novak worked for to England. Once there, Josef and Hertha immediately remarried and Josef adopted his own children! About a year later, the Novak family obtained visas to the United States, no doubt aided by rich influential American sponsors who had known Professor Novak while they were still in Vienna.

Once in New York, there was one more hurdle to overcome. Any foreign doctor with an MD certificate other than American had to undergo an examination proving that he was really fit to practice medicine in the United States. Josef presented himself to an examiner who immediately asked, "Are you by any chance related to the Josef Novak who wrote the book about gynecology that we are using?"

"I am the Josef Novak, the person who wrote the book," Josef replied.

The examiner immediately got up and shook Josef's hand.

"Well," he said, "we in America are so happy to have a physician such as you with us. You need no test."

Of his three daughters, the youngest one, Gertrude, was of special interest to us. She entered medical school at a very young age and graduated while still in her early twenties. She became, after a few years, the chief of pathology at Cook County Hospital in Chicago.

My family and I had moved to Skokie, a suburb of Chicago, where Gertrude visited us frequently. Professor Novak retired from medical practice when he reached the good age of eighty and moved to Chicago to live with his daughter. His beloved wife, Hertha, had died while they were still in New York.

On his 100th birthday, Josef Novak was honored by the Austrian Consulate in Chicago as one of the most prominent Austrians alive. A little later Gertrude and her father came to visit us. We lived in a house with a backyard where I had planted not only grass but also a little vegetable garden. Josef, Gertrude, my wife, our daughters and I went for a walk in our backyard. My daughter, Linda, at that time may have been about ten years old.

Suddenly Josef Novak stopped walking and bent down all the way to the ground. Needless to say we were all scared — a 100-year-old man bending down like that! But Josef knew what he was doing. He had seen a little bug struggling to get off its back after falling off the edge of the grass and into the vegetable garden.

Josef very gently took the bug between his thumb and finger and put it back into the grass. I couldn't help remembering my mother's words, "He has such gentle hands!"

WITH A FOREIGN ACCENT

(Excerpts selected by Otto Schnepp)

INTRODUCTION

In 1941, my wife, Teri, and I were in hiding from the Germans in a rented room in Bratislava, the capital of Slovakia that Germany had split off from Czechoslovakia. A rumor spread that the Nazis were going to move in soon. Jews were again in danger.

Fortunately, Teri held a Hungarian passport in her maiden name which allowed her to move freely within Slovakia, Germany, and Hungary, her parents' home. However, it would expire in a month, and she had to return to Hungary to renew it. We had our American visa ready for issuance at the U.S. Consulate in Budapest, the capital of Hungary, due to the efforts of my brother who lived in Chicago. Moreover, I had been living and working in Bratislava illegally. There was no legal way for me to cross the border from Slovakia. We had to separate. We hugged and parted. Teri was calm, but I feared that we might never meet again.

JANOSH

I made efforts to learn as much as possible about the border and where to cross it with the best chances for success. I was advised that the mountains of eastern Slovakia were not heavily patrolled. This was several weeks before the Germans invaded the Soviet Union, and Eastern

Europe was still peaceful. The Jews were persecuted in Slovakia under German pressure, but the Slovaks were not rabid anti-Semites. I also learned that a Jewish family named Hirsch lived close to the point where I planned to cross the border, and they would help me. Their house was located high in the mountains, a full day's walk from the nearest railway station.

I took a night train, arriving early in the morning at the designated station and started on my hike to the Hirsch's house, carrying all my possessions in a backpack. I climbed uphill on a deserted narrow dirt road which led through a forest. Soon I passed the tree line and was now on the path overlooking a deep ravine. As I looked at the road on the opposite side of the ravine, I saw a soldier walking towards a waterfall where we would meet. Encountering a border patrol was just what I had dreaded. I assumed that the soldier had already seen me. If he arrested me, the authorities would send me back to Germany and most likely to a concentration camp. Fear gripped me. For a moment I considered running back into the forest, but I had been told that these border patrols were usually mean, trigger-happy soldiers. I would be an easy target. I considered another possibility: perhaps I could simply walk to meet the soldier and then try to push him down into the ravine. I was physically strong and a surprise attack might succeed. But this plan was not acceptable to me; I was not comfortable with violence. I decided to keep on walking and somehow try to talk the soldier out of arresting me.

We met on a small bridge above the waterfall where both sides of the ravine met. The soldier shouted, *"Na straz!"* This was the patriotic greeting in the new state of Slovakia, the local equivalent of *Heil Hitler*, although the literal meaning is "watch out." I decided that it was not a good idea to return the same greeting and just wished him a good morning.

"What are you doing here?" the soldier asked. He spoke with an east Slovak accent. I spoke Slovak well at the time, although my speech was closer to the west Slovak, the official language of the country.

"I am a tourist," I replied. "I have my backpack, as you see, and I love this beautiful country."

"Beautiful country, my ass! Don't you know that you are near the border? You have no business walking around here. I should arrest you."

I managed to stay cool. "But I have business here. I am visiting my friend, Mr. Hirsch."

"Don't bullshit me. You don't even know the Hirsch Jews."

I was at a loss for a reply. The soldier's pink face reddened with excitement. I decided to wait for the border guard to speak.

"Show me your passport!" he commanded after some hesitation. He probably had remembered his standard instructions.

"Sure, I'll get it out right away," I said, and I slowly opened my backpack to extract the passport and handed it to the soldier.

"So you have a German passport?" He had obviously recognized the swastika, the emblem of Slovakia's big neighbor and protector.

"Yes," I replied.

As the soldier inspected the photograph on the inside of the document, a sheet of paper fell out. He picked it up and studied it with intense concentration. It also bore a photograph.

"This is from the German army, sir?" he finally asked, having switched to a more polite tone. He obviously had recognized the words "*Deutsche Wehrmacht*," the German equivalent of "German Army" which appeared frequently in the Slovak papers.

"Yes, it is," I replied, trying to avoid going into detail.

"What does it say, sir?" the soldier inquired.

The moment of truth had arrived and I decided to play it straight.

"It says "*UNTAUGLICH DA JUDE*," which means 'unfit for army service as a Jew.'"

It turned out that this Slovak soldier, this peasant boy stuck in a uniform, had a great sense of the ridiculous. He laughed and laughed. Then he put his rifle on the ground, slapped his thighs with both hands and laughed some more.

"You are a Jew? Funny, funny! That is why you want to visit the Hirsch Jews! I thought that you are a spy, with your learned stupid city accent that only my teacher had. Nobody speaks like this around here. I thought that maybe you are a Russian, you know. Of course we are at peace with the Ruskies, but I don't trust them, and their country is now only a few kilometers from here. So you are not a spy, you are only a Jew. Funny! But what the hell are you really doing here?" The soldier was laughing all the way.

I was encouraged by the man's good humor and answered truthfully, "I want to go to America, and I have to pick up my visa in Hungary."

"Sure," the soldier interrupted, "You are a smart man. You know, my mother keeps telling me I should go to America.

'Janosh,' she says, 'don't trust the Germans, don't trust the Russians, don't trust the shitty Hungarians in the next valley. Don't trust anybody.'"

"But you have your own country now," I replied. I did not know what to make of the soldier's confidences. I thought it best to be careful and flatter him.

"Bullshit. We farmers will get screwed one way or the other. The guys in the capital who are running our country now don't even talk like we do. They talk like my teacher did. Of course, if I go to America, I'd have to learn the American language. My Uncle Milosh writes it is quite difficult. It doesn't sound anything like Slovak or even Hungarian."

It was nice chatting with this fellow, I thought, but I really needed to get on. Actually, I was still not certain that the guard would let me go. Again I decided to try the direct approach.

"Is it still far to the Hungarian border?" I asked.

"No, a couple of hours." He started to laugh again. "You and the Hirsch Jews! Old man Hirsch has a beard all the way down to his belt, and he always wears a hat. You don't look like him at all! How come you are a Jew, too? Anyway, I went to school with his younger son, a smart fellow, and strong! He beat me at arm wrestling every time. But let me tell you, I can shoot better than he can. Nobody can shoot like me. Bet I can hit a bird flying high in the sky!"

I congratulated myself on my decision not to attempt flight.

"Well," the Slovak prattled on, "if you really want to stop by to see the Hirshes, you cannot miss them. Just go straight ahead on this road for about an hour and you will see their house. Tell them Janosh sends his greetings. By the way, let me tell you, be careful the Hungarian border guards don't catch you. Those bastards are mean! They will beat you with their rifles! I get along with them, of course. I speak their shitty language, but they don't know a single word of Slovak. They are real stupid. They cannot even catch the gypsies who cross the border all night right under their noses smuggling coffee and tea. When I catch them, I beat them up but good. They should work like I do. By the way, I hope that you don't have anything like that in your backpack."

I assured the guard that I only carried personal belongings and opened my backpack for inspection. The soldier was satisfied, but he had opened a side pocket and found the picture of my wife, Teri.

"She sure is pretty," he said. "Is she already in America?"

"No, she is waiting for me in Hungary."

"Oh well, then don't keep her waiting any longer. Maybe we will meet some time in America if I ever decide to join my uncle."

The Slovak looked down at the waterfall. "But much water will flow until then," he said wistfully. "Meanwhile, I hope I will not get into the war." He stretched out his hand to me. "You better go now. Be careful and good luck," he added, and as a final gesture of goodwill he gave me the traditional Slovak farewell, "*S' Bohom* (God be with you)."

I took his hand and shook it. "*S' Bohom*," I replied and was off, much relieved to have survived a major threat.

GYPSIES

I had no difficulty finding the Hirsch's house. An elderly man was sitting in front, skullcap on his head, engrossed in his afternoon prayers. He paid no attention to me.

A young man appeared from inside. "You must be the man who wants to cross the border tonight," he said. "They wrote me about you from Bratislava. You are lucky the patrol didn't catch you."

"He did. Janosh sends you his greetings." I related my adventure.

"So, you and Janosh had a little fun!" The young man, who did not look all that different from Janosh, laughed.

"Have a bite to eat, rest a while. We'll depart in an hour, after the sun sets."

The old man completed his prayers and gave me the traditional Hebrew greeting, "*Shalom Aleichem.*" It was all he said to me before disappearing into the house.

The young man, presumably the son of Mr. Hirsch, said, "The Jewish community in Bratislava pays me for every man I get across the border, but it is very little." Then he added, "You have a nice wristwatch. Maybe you won't need it anymore?"

I took the not-too-subtle hint and handed the watch over to my presumed guide. The watch had been a present from my mother and therefore had sentimental value. However, I felt justified in sacrificing it for the sake of my safety. "By all means have it," was all I said.

I was not sure I liked or trusted this fellow. He soon brought me a plate with a few hot potatoes. The simple meal was most welcome since I had not eaten all day and further exertions were yet to come, I assumed.

We left at dusk, first crossing a pass between two hills and then following a sloping path downhill. A few huts were now visible.

"Are we already in Hungary?" I asked.

"Oh no, we are still in Slovakia. But all you have to do now is to go down to this gypsy camp. They know you are coming, and they will take you to Hungary!"

"But I thought that you are my guide!" I called out with some trepidation.

"No. Just go, fast! I have to leave." He disappeared without another word.

I felt betrayed and abandoned by this young man, who, after all, had said that he had been paid for taking me across the border. But at this point I had no choice but to take my chances with the gypsies.

I entered the only hut that was lit, and about a dozen men greeted me enthusiastically. I suspected that they were more than a little inebriated. They obviously had been expecting me, but I did not understand a word they said. They were speaking Hungarian!

"Do you speak Slovak?" I asked in that language, "or German?"

They just laughed in response. "*Magyarul* (Hungarian)!"

After a while one of the men spoke up in a language approximating English, "I was America. Work hard. Bad country."

I soon realized that my hopes of having found somebody I could talk to had been dashed. Obviously, this man had exhausted his English vocabulary. After much loud conversation and laughing, another man pointed at himself, then at me and said "*Magyarorszag*" (Hungary).

I understood that he would be my guide. But when I

gathered up my backpack, the guide motioned that it was too heavy and must be left behind. Well, I was in no position to argue.

The two of us left the hut. The guide handed me a small bag to carry, and he, himself, carried on his back a large bag which was obviously quite heavy. There was no doubt that this man was a smuggler. I was anxious. What if the Hungarian or Slovak border guards caught us, I thought. Not only were we crossing the border illegally, but we were also smuggling!

As we made our way in the dark, the guide suddenly pulled me down, whispering, "*Katonag!*" I did not understand the word but soon realized that the gypsy must have spied soldiers. After a long while, perhaps a whole hour, the guide motioned to me that the coast was clear, and we could continue on our way. Not long afterwards, the guide pulled me down hard to the ground again. He must have seen somebody once more. I did not see anything in the pitch black night and felt utterly powerless. I was completely dependent on the gypsy guide for my safety and, indeed, my survival. The same routine was repeated many times during the next several hours. Go on, get down, forward again. I was beginning to feel very tired. But, finally, we reached a highway just as the day dawned.

"*Magyarorszag!*" the guide exclaimed, took the bag I had carried for him, shook hands with me, pointed at the highway for me to follow and disappeared. Great relief flooded me. I had survived another dangerous step in my struggle to reach America.

KASSA, HUNGARY

I had followed the road for only a few minutes when I saw a railway station and my father-in-law standing in front of it with a big shawl in his hands. What a welcome sight that was! He motioned for me to be quiet, hugged me and wrapped the shawl around my head and chin.

"You have a bad cold, you are hoarse, you cannot talk at all," my father-in-law, Mr. Vidor, whispered in my ear. His eyes welcomed me, but nothing further was said, as long as we were within earshot of other people. I did not speak Hungarian, and we might have attracted attention, if we spoke another language. We boarded a train which soon arrived, but again we observed silence. Eventually, the train pulled into the station in Kassa where the Vidor family lived, and we walked to their home, a few minutes away. Teri was there, waiting for him as were her mother and sister. We all hugged, laughed and cried with joy and relief.

A few days later a buggy pulled up at the gate of the house, and I recognized the gypsy who spoke a few words of English. Without saying a word, the gypsy threw the backpack I had left behind, on the sidewalk and vanished. I was taken aback by the honesty of these gypsies!

Not speaking Hungarian, I had to keep silent when not at home. There was one exception. The Vidors had a dry goods store and during market days, twice a week, I was asked to act as cashier. At those times, the store was always full of customers, all Slovak farm women from the surrounding hills of Kassa. These farmers only spoke Slovak. They liked me and joked with me.

"So you are the new man; be sure to marry one of the Vidor girls," one of the women customers would say. "Don't live in sin!" Or, "I'd gladly give my money to such a nice young fellow," another would say. And again: "Look, I did NOT steal this piece of cloth, not this time, anyway!"

Business was good, and the Vidors prospered. In retrospect, this was unfortunate. The Hungarian Jews did not have any incentive to think of leaving. They had no inkling of what was in store for them when the Hungarian Nazis would take over in 1943, and most of the Jews of Hungary were deported to concentration camps where very few survived.

In 1941, when I was there, Hungary felt like a nice and free country. Life was good in spite of the German invasion of the Soviet Union which was just a few hundred miles to the east. Teri and I frequently went to the local swimming pool or for long walks. We were free to be very much in love.

In July Teri and I received our American visa. This was an occasion for celebration, except that we did not see any possibility of getting out of Europe. We were surrounded on all sides by Germany and by war. A few months earlier we might have been able to reach America by way of Siberia and Japan. However, by July, Hungary and all her neighbors were directly involved in the war after Germany's invasion of Russia. We were trapped. The American visa for which we had been anxiously waiting since 1938 now seemed useless.

BRÜNHILDE

One day, out of the blue, we heard a rumor at the Jewish Community Center in Budapest that a most unlikely route might be open to us: through Germany, occupied France and Spain. This plan sounded strange, bordering on the absurd. I had succeeded in evading

Germany, and now we might find a way out by going back. However, it did not seem credible that the Germans would allow us to pass through their country. But still, we accepted it as our duty to pursue all possibilities. Also, I was in Hungary illegally and might be picked up by the police at any moment. There was no time to lose!

We had been told to contact a German agency, the HAPAG, which, prior to the war had been charged with shipping freight from Hamburg, Germany, to New York. Since the outbreak of war with Great Britain in 1939, no German freighters or passenger ships sailed the Atlantic, nor did any U.S. ships call at German ports, even though the U.S. was a neutral power. But the HAPAG office in Budapest still existed, and one morning in July 1941, Teri and I went there. We had rehearsed our parts well in advance. Teri would do the talking if Hungarian was the current language, and I would be the spokesman if German was required.

We found the office closed with a sign indicating the business hours to be from 2:00 p.m. to 4:30 p.m. When we returned shortly after 2:00, we entered and found a young man behind the counter speaking to a customer in Hungarian. But there also was an older woman, probably in her early sixties, sitting in a separate office in the back. We guessed that she was the senior person in charge. She was also busy, negotiating in German with two important-looking gentlemen. We just stood there, waiting to be recognized.

After about ten minutes the woman waved to us to approach. Her grimace and her off-putting hand gesture conveyed contempt. We had a good look at her now: she was stout and tall with long, unkempt grey hair falling over her shoulders. She reminded me of Richard Wagner's operatic character, Brünhilde, but aged and wasted.

"What do you want?" she barked at us in German. I was surprised that she did not use Hungarian, the local language.

I began by telling her that we had heard of HAPAG procuring transportation for Jews who want to emigrate from Europe. I did not get any further.

"You goddamned Jews," the woman interrupted in a screechy scream. "What makes you think I would waste my time on you! I am talking to more important people now! Maybe I might see you at 6 o'clock but now get out of here before I kick your ass!" The two gentlemen just watched.

Teri and I left in shock. Taking stock, there were many things that did not make sense. Why had the woman screamed at us and cursed us? She had rudely thrown us out but then had said that she might talk to us at 6 o'clock or after the posted office hours. Perhaps she would ask for a bribe when she would be alone with us. But then, why was she so rude and mean?

We decided that we had no choice but to return at 6 p.m. We peeked through the window before entering. "Brünhilde" was at her post, but the young man was no longer there. Ready for the worst, we entered, trembling. To our surprise and relief, the woman got up from her chair, stretched out both arms and addressed us in a friendly voice.

"Welcome! I am so glad you came back. I was afraid that you would not return. Please excuse my behavior this afternoon. I had to do it for appearance's sake; it is a show I am forced to put on for those people!" With a gesture of her hand, she indicated her contempt for those people. "Sit down," she said politely, in a mellow voice, now really reminding me of an opera singer. "Tell me about yourselves. I can probably help."

She was no prettier than before, but now she looked more like a friendly grandmother who was too busy with her grandchildren to take care of herself. I was too surprised and moved by this turn of events to be able to speak. Teri recovered first and explained that we finally had received our American visas, but we were at a loss as to how to get out of Europe.

The woman turned to address me. "Earlier today, you spoke German perfectly well, but your wife speaks it with a Hungarian accent. What is your nationality?"

I told the woman that I was born and raised in Vienna and had first an Austrian and now a German passport. We also now would be able to travel on a "stateless document" and were in Budapest solely to obtain our American visa.

"Don't tell me how you got to Hungary, I don't want to know that," she replied. "They are treating you dreadfully but, believe me, it will get much worse. You should get out as fast as you can; all Jews should. Right now you have a good chance."

The woman explained that she was in the process of collecting the names of all Jews now residing in Hungary and who had a visa from any country overseas. Once a week she sent a list to Berlin requesting transportation to Spain. She had to assure her contact in Berlin that she had personally interviewed the people, that they were not wanted by the German police and owed no German taxes. It was in the interest of Germany to get such people out so that there would be fewer Jews in Europe, she explained. The route we would follow would lead from Budapest to Munich by train and from there to Madrid by plane. The cost and fees would be payable on receipt of the travel permit and the appropriate tickets.

"You see, the wind is blowing from the right direction in Berlin, as far as you are concerned, but this will only be for a short time. I implore you, hurry! It will not be long before terrible things will happen to all European Jews. It is already very bad in Poland, but it will get much worse very soon."

We worked in the HAPAG office under the guidance of "Brünhilde" (we never learned her real name) for over an hour. There were reams of forms to be filled out; the Germans are fond of paper. The slightest error or omission would be cause for "Berlin" to reject our application. I asked the woman how long it might take to receive permission to leave.

"You will be on the sixth list; I already have received the first three lists approved by the authorities. You should get the good news in about four weeks, God willing."

As we left the HAPAG office, we thanked the old lady profusely and heard her mumble something like, "This is the least I can do as a German woman."

We felt on top of the world. In four weeks we could be on our way to freedom and safety. The woman had not said anything that could be construed as a request for a bribe. She had not even asked for a down payment on the travel!

"Now you might as well start learning English," I said to Teri on the train back to Kassa.

"It looks like I might need it!" Teri agreed.

UNDER ARREST

"*J̄oregelt kivanok!*" A voice woke me from a sound sleep on a couch in my in-laws' apartment in Kassa. I knew only about a hundred words of Hungarian and these included the greeting, "I wish you good morning." I thought it safe to repeat the greeting.

However, as I opened my eyes I found myself facing a policeman staring at me. What I had feared for several months had finally come to pass. I was to be arrested for being in Hungary illegally.

"I am afraid you have to get dressed quickly." My father-in-law was now talking to me in German. "Mother has already awakened Teri."

I looked at the clock on the wall: it was 5 o'clock in the morning.

"But Teri is a Hungarian citizen! She is not subject to arrest," I mumbled.

"The police don't think so," Mr. Vidor responded, and I saw tears in his eyes. Teri was his oldest daughter, the apple of his eye. "Because she is married to you she is now considered a German citizen, like you."

Oh my God, I thought. I had believed all this time that Teri was safe in her father's house. Jews had hardly been bothered so far in Hungary as long as they were Hungarian citizens. We had been married in faraway Prague two years earlier because this was the only way Teri could register together with me for emigration to America. Except for the in-laws, there was nobody in all of Hungary who knew that we were married. The American consulate in Budapest must have contacted the local police, for whatever reason.

As I dressed, I saw Teri who was, as usual, her calm self.

"They'll let us go as soon as they see our American visas," she said encouragingly.

The mother joined us, crying. "Why couldn't you have stayed in Budapest for just another day? They would never have found you there."

The policeman spoke up again and somebody translated for my benefit, "I'm sorry to do this. I have nothing against German Jews. But my orders are to take you to the local high school. I must also ask you to take warm clothes. You will be transported to Siberia."

In spite of the dreadful situation I had to laugh at this pronouncement. The Germans had invaded Russia just two months earlier. They and their Hungarian allies could hardly have progressed as far as Siberia by then!

An hour later we joined a group of about 15 people in one of the classrooms of the high school, and more kept coming. We talked and commiserated. Eventually a policeman of higher rank entered and made a short speech in Hungarian. Teri translated for my benefit. The police officer had explained that "many important personalities" were working for the release of the detainees, and he advised patience. As a matter of fact, nobody seemed to be very upset. There was much laughter, and they joked a lot to while away the time. A short man even was giving advice to Hitler. "He made a mistake, he should have asked me. Instead of invading Russia he should have tried Italy. It is warmer there and the wine is better!"

Suddenly, the good-humored banter was interrupted by a scream from an elderly lady, "You fools, don't you realize that we're all going to perish in Siberia? I'll never see my grandchildren again!"

At noon a policeman brought sandwiches and coffee,

which had been brought by the relatives of the arrested, he explained. During all the commotion Teri kept calm and did not participate in the frenzied joking nor in the hysterical screaming. At 4 o'clock in the afternoon she whispered to me:

"I only hope that we will be able to stay together. My father will do everything in his power to get us out. But I am afraid!"

Teri was interrupted by the higher ranking police officer who made a short announcement in Hungarian. I did not have to wait for a translation. Everybody got up, picked up their suitcases and quietly marched out of the school to a waiting bus. It seemed to us that half the town was watching. The bus started off in a northeasterly direction towards Poland.

Half an hour later, the bus stopped, and we all descended. Teri and I were separated, without a chance to say goodbye. All the men were loaded onto a train which continued in a similar direction for another two hours.

After we descended from the train, the arrested men were taken to a makeshift camp near a Hungarian town surrounded by beautiful wooded hills. This camp was in no way comparable to the concentration camps run by Germans or Austrians. There were no watchtowers, no barbed wire. Only wooden fences surrounded the camp. The inmates could easily have wandered off into the surrounding forests as only one bored policeman was on watch. Living quarters were in half-finished huts with straw for beds. Except for fleas and bed bugs we all slept peacefully. There was a kitchen somewhere on the grounds staffed by older soldiers who prepared edible food in sufficient quantity to keep the inmates from feeling hungry.

No work was required of us, not even finishing the huts was ordered, although we would have been motivated to do such work for fear of what the winter would be like.

I asked to see the commander of the camp who showed up every few days. He received me, was polite and spoke to me in broken German. However, he showed no interest in my American visa. "I have no orders for you other than to keep you here," he said. "No idea how long you will be kept here. A lot of places, not many kilometers from here, are much worse than this camp. I hope you get to America. If you do, tell the Americans that we Hungarians are good people, not like the others."

The inmates of the camp organized activities to keep themselves occupied. I taught English for beginners, and I took lessons from another man who was more advanced. We played chess on improvised boards, and there even was a man who told bible stories, complete with commentaries. All of us were afraid of being shipped to Poland, as had already happened to many Czech Jews. More important to me, I had not had any news of Teri. Had she never met me, I thought, she would have been safe in her father's house.

Three weeks went by and then, on a hot August day, I was called to the camp commander.

"I have orders to let you go," he said in his broken German. "Since you have an American visa, we won't hold you here any longer. Your wife is also being released. I'll even give you papers, which will keep you from being arrested again. But you must hurry, there is only one more train out of here today. The station is six kilometers from here."

I wanted to thank the commander, but he interrupted. "Be sure to tell the Americans that we Hungarians are decent people," he enjoined me once again.

I parted from my fellow inmates, hurriedly packed my suitcase and ran most of the way to the station. The August sun was hot on me, and I also had to carry my heavy suitcase! I was fortunate to catch the train and by evening I was back in Kassa. I walked to the Vidors' home where I found Teri, who had been released one day earlier.

By then, I was so exhausted that I could barely embrace and kiss Teri. I collapsed and fell asleep on the living room carpet, unable to stand up any longer.

As in a dream, I heard Teri say: "The sixth list has arrived from Germany. We can now go to America."

ANOTHER HURDLE

We were excited. It was August 1941, and we had our American visas, good for entry until October 1. Equally important, the German authorities in Berlin had sent us transit visas to travel through Germany. Being in Hungary, with war raging all around us, this was the only possible way out to the west. With the transit visas we had been given the complete routing and tickets, all at a comparatively reasonable price. Our travel was to take us by train from Budapest to Vienna and on to Munich. Then we were to continue by plane across France to Madrid. Franco Spain remained neutral throughout the war. Then all we needed was passage across the Atlantic.

We never understood what motivated the Nazis to treat us so well. In retrospect, it all seems like a miracle! After all, they gave us, two Jews, extremely scarce airplane seats, something reserved at that time for high level officials and diplomats. One possible theory might be that the German Foreign Ministry wanted to influence the U.S. to stay out of the war.

In an elated mood, we went to the Spanish Consulate in Budapest to apply for a transit visa. We assumed that this would be a mere formality, since we could not be suspected of wishing to stay in Franco's Spain.

An official, a woman, carefully examined the family travel document with the American visa and seemed pleased. "Good, you are going to America," she said in Hungarian. "And how do you plan to travel to Madrid?"

Teri, who carried on the conversation, showed the official the German travel documents and tickets. "I believe that you will find these papers all in order," she said. "Aren't we lucky?" Teri translated the gist of the conversation into German for my benefit.

"You have your ship tickets, of course?" The woman said to me in broken German.

"Well, practically," I explained. "As soon as we get to Madrid we will wire my brother in Chicago and he will then send us the tickets."

I produced my brother's letter explaining the circumstances. "Since transatlantic ship accommodations are scarce, the actual tickets will only be issued to persons already in Spain. Otherwise, the shipping line cannot be certain that the prospective users will actually reach the Spanish port of departure," my brother had written.

The lady's face, so pleasant until then, turned stern. "I am sorry, but we cannot issue a Spanish transit visa under these conditions. As you know, Mr. Franco is very kind to Jews, but too many Jews are already in Spain and are stuck there. His Excellency, the Consul, has received instructions directly from the Caudillo not to issue any transit visas to Jews unless they are already in possession of ship tickets. Come back when you have them," the woman said with a tone of finality. She had referred to Franco by his official title, meaning "Leader," equivalent to the German "Führer" which Hitler used.

Nowadays such a situation would be called a "catch 22." I could not see my way out of this dilemma. Just to be sure, I again wired my brother, but received the same reply as before.

It was Mr. Vidor, Teri's father, who came up with a strategy which promised success. Drawing on his extensive experience gleaned from long years of doing business in Central Europe, he did two things.

First, he sent a cable to a travel agency in Budapest whose owner was an acquaintance with the following text: "Have transatlantic tickets for Mr. & Mrs. Weinman from Spanish port to New York. Stop. American Express."

Second, he sent a letter to the home address of the lady official at the Spanish consulate. I do not know how he obtained the address. In this letter, written in especially flowery Hungarian (as Teri explained to me), Mr. Vidor thanked her for the excellent reception she had extended to his children. He stressed that these "children" (24 years and 27 years old) were still rather inexperienced and therefore the information she had so generously given them was all the more welcome. In order to show his appreciation, he was taking the extraordinary liberty, for which he begged forgiveness, of sending her a bolt of the best English fabric, good for a fine suit. He added that he had been the representative of a large English mill and still had some material from that source in stock. If the fabric might find favor in her eyes, the letter continued, he would be more than happy to send her another bolt of fabric from which any good tailor could make an overcoat to protect her from the harsh Hungarian winter.

Mr. Vidor assumed that the nice lady at the Spanish consulate might have considerable influence, in which case a small gift as well as the promise of more to come would be helpful. We waited for a few days to make sure that the bolt of fabric had time to arrive and then we returned to the Spanish consulate. We had decided to let Teri address the lady since they had determined that she was more comfortable speaking Hungarian. As soon as we were recognized, the official gave us a meaningful look from which we surmised that the bolt of fabric had indeed "found favor in her eyes."

Teri handed the woman the fake telegram, which we had picked up at the travel agency. She also made a small speech, which I did not understand, but Teri told me later that it was full of extremely polite expressions, such as exist only in the Hungarian language. The official looked at the telegram, turned it over, then put it on her desk, looked at each of us in turn, and then said to Teri in a low voice, "*Az semmi.*"

I understood just enough Hungarian to know what this meant. "This is nothing." The three of us just stood there in silence. I looked at Teri and my heart missed a beat.

After what felt like an eternity, but probably was in reality not more than ten seconds, the lady turned to me. She was breathing hard. "I will take this 'telegram,'" the tone of her voice when she pronounced the word and her grimace made it clear what she thought of it, "to the Consul anyway. I think His Excellency is having a good day. Maybe, just maybe…

Give me your passport."

She disappeared into the interior of the consular offices and we sat down on a bench, holding hands. Anxiety gripped us.

The official returned in no time, holding our passport over her head, smiling. "His Excellency signed your visa! He was concentrating on something important. I said to him, 'Just sign here' and he did. Congratulations!"

Teri thanked the woman in flowery Hungarian, I added my thanks in German and then added, just for good luck, "Muchas gracias!" You bet your life, the lady received the second bolt of fabric!

From then on, everything went smoothly. Parting from Teri's parents was really difficult. As it turned out, this was the last time we saw them. They were cruelly murdered.

We were allowed to buy ten dollars in American currency and that was all the money we had to cover our expenses until we boarded the ship in Bilbao. Fortunately, my brother, Charles, had had the foresight to send us five twenty-dollar bills in a letter, care of the American Express, Madrid. We were rich!

We arrived in New York on October 12, 1941, Columbus Day, after having survived a scary storm at sea, our very last hurdle before reaching U.S. shores. We went on to Chicago a few days later. There, Charles was waiting for us at the station. Was that ever a happy reunion!

NOTE: *Frank and Teri immigrated to Chicago where he worked for a manufacturer of decals, along with his brother, a Ph.D. chemist who had arrived three years earlier. After Pearl Harbor, Frank continued in this job, having been classified as an essential worker for the war effort. He retired in 1980. Widowed twice, he has two daughters with families in California — hence his move to Rossmoor. With A Foreign Accent tells of his European youth, along with many short stories. Referring to his writing once, he remarked to his classmates, "I don't want to make myself more interesting than I really am." They appreciate his critiques of their work— incisive, witty and often from a decidedly different point of view.*

 *MILTON MATZ, as always, is dressed as if going to a university to lecture. He reminds me of a professor and that is rather close to the truth. He is a rabbi as well as a clinical psychologist. His stories are in the form of plays, and he reads with calmness and deliberation. He makes no mention of the fact that they are based on knowledge of what his family went through. His demeanor does not change as he begins to read.*

FREDDY

REDDY is a story about love, pitting a man against destiny. The play, one scene, ten minutes in length requires a cast of two, a man and a woman. A single unit set is adequate.

Cast of characters

Freddy: A Jewish physician in his middle forties.
Wiltrude: Freddy's wife, a nurse, in her early forties.

Time: December, 1940
Setting: Freddy's examining room in his Berlin apartment

As the play opens, Freddy is seated at a small desk facing the audience. A medical examining table is to his left. A chair is in front of the examining table. Pen in hand he is writing a letter. He reads each word as he slowly writes. Every word and phrase is a struggle.

FREDDY: My dearest one, Forgive me! I plan to take three capsules of Veronal, because I see this as the only way out for you and the children. Very difficult it is for me to take this step, but finally I have found the courage to face the fact that this is necessary. But I waited until today not to disturb you and the children during the holidays. It was for me a question of morality, is it right for me to kill myself? But, I decided it is my duty. When I'm gone, it will be easier for you to survive. Call Dr. Alfred Grock and ask him to issue a "regular" death certificate. Tell him to shade the truth if that is possible. I believe that is easier to bear for you and the children. There is probably no other way. When your husband is removed, everything hopefully will be all right. Hug and kiss the children for me. And you, I kiss passionately, your tearful Freddy.
Passionately, Your Freddy
(He quietly studies the letter for a moment. WILTRUDE enters the room and he quickly hides the letter in the drawer of the desk.)

WILTRUDE: *(Without a word she pulls the empty chair over to FREDDY. She looks at him and hugs him.)*

You can't sleep, also? Can I get you some tea? I need some.

FREDDY: I don't want to bother you. You must be exhausted.

WILTRUDE: Do we have a choice? The Germans may come any day to take us away. It could be tomorrow or next week or... in half an hour.

FREDDY: Or this morning!

WILTRUDE: I have been trying to think of some other way. I keep coming back to my idea. I think it's worth a try.

FREDDY: It will never work. We will all get killed.

WILTRUDE: What if the superintendent overlooks the matter. Suppose he thinks the matter can be kept from the Gestapo by hiding the report.

FREDDY: Not Grossman. I know his mind. If he knows of a violation of Gestapo rules, he will not keep it from the Gestapo. He will be scrupulously honest. That is how he has remained the Jewish director of the Berlin Jewish Hospital all these years. He will never endanger himself.

WILTRUDE: If he knows of a violation. What if he doesn't find out? What if he drinks too much again and forgets to look at the end of the month reports. He may miss your diagnosis of Dr. Bremmer.

FREDDY: I saw the monthly papers on his desk. My diagnoses were there. It is only a matter of time. I didn't think he would check this month. But his secretary said, she risked her life, she said, that he asked for all the diagnoses for this month, and he is particularly checking and re-examining all patients who were diagnosed as too ill for transport.

WILTRUDE: What if he decides to overlook it? He is your friend. Just like you are Dr. Bremmer's friend.

FREDDY: Not like I am Dr. Bremmer's friend. I should have been like Grossman. I should have said Bremmer is fully recovered from his suicide attempt. He is healthier than I am. He is healthy enough to be deported.

WILTRUDE: Why didn't you write that?

FREDDY: God forgive me. I wanted to write that. But at the last moment I couldn't. I wrote, "His heart is too weak to survive the trip." I put my family under the axe! My two small children! I could strangle myself.

WILTRUDE: Would Bremmer have risked himself for you?

FREDDY: I am not sure? Who knows? We were in medical school together… I don't know?

WILTRUDE: How much time do we have?

FREDDY: Till the next transport. They are going out every month now. I think we have till the end of the month. But no longer.

WILTRUDE: How will we know when they plan to pick us up? Will they tell us?

FREDDY: Yes, they will tell us. By a loud, very loud, knock on the door early in the morning of the next transport. And then it will be too late for us to do anything except march... like sheep. But there is one thing I can do which can save you and the children. And I must do it before that loud knock on the door.

WILTRUDE: I don't want you to kill yourself.

FREDDY: I must. But, they must not see my death as suicide. They will see it, with Dr. Grock's help, as a normal death. As a normal death, not an escape or a suicide, they will not pay special attention to you and the children. With a little bit of luck they will not look into the religion of the children.

WILTRUDE: I don't want to split up the family. It's better we escape together and stay together... even if we all perish! To me that's the most important thing... that we stay together, that the family stays together. Together we will overcome everything.

FREDDY: It is all my fault. I am the Jew. I insisted our children be registered as Jews. I falsified Brenner's diagnosis. I can atone and save my family... by taking my life. And I can do so with courage.

WILTRUDE: Enough with your nobility. I need you to be with me. The Gestapo knows the children are Jewish. That's a pipe dream that the children will escape detection. After you kill yourself the children will be picked up as Jews. And if they don't pick me up with them, I will insist I go with them! Could I leave them to go alone? And then what would your suicide accomplish? Who knows, all of us going with the transport together could be better than suicide.

FREDDY: The best outcome is for me to die. At least three can escape.

WILTRUDE: The best outcome is my aunt's house. All four could possibly escape.

FREDDY: We have to make a decision soon. Time is running short. If we don't choose, the Gestapo makes the decision.

WILTRUDE: My decision is made. My aunt! But the final decision is in your hands. I pray, choose the family... But, if we never meet again... No! Please choose the family!... But, if we never meet again...
(She kisses him tenderly.)

NOTE: *Milton is an award winning playwright and he believes the Holocaust has exerted a life-long impact on all his work. A founder of the Pastoral Psychology Institute at Case-Western Reserve School of Medicine, he guided it into becoming the largest and most successful interfaith clinical continuing education program for clergy of the nation. The Hebrew Union College awarded him an honorary doctorate for his work on conflict resolution in family, business, and religious settings.*

LEN MORGENSTERN is a retired Kaiser pathologist and published author of many computer-related articles. Learning of his Canadian cousin's war ordeals, he journeyed there to record them — and how apropos that twenty years later they became a part of this collection.

MANNES (MORRIS) BERLINER
1922—1999

I interviewed Mannes in Winnipeg in 1989. A full transcription is on my website: www. leonardmorgenstern.com. Mannes spoke very good English, almost accent-free, peppered by frequent "you knows," occasionally several to a sentence. Often his thinking would get ahead of his speech.

The result was usually perfectly understandable to the ear but can look confused on the page. I have edited where necessary, but I have let a few examples remain as they were said.

BEFORE THE WAR

MANNIE: You see, what really happened, our town was really, literally, the first victim of the Germans. You see, we lived on the border of Germany and East Prussia, and the whole town lived out of the border trade. You see, it was a Polish-German border, and it was an open border, the same as between Canada and the United States. And most of the people, like my father, had a partnership with Germans. And they used to bring stuff, an international trade. And, of course, some was legal, some was illegal, but everybody made a living. As a matter of fact, the whole town was considered well off in those days.

As soon as Hitler came to power [1933], the border closed. So, in other words, the town got cut off from their source of income, and overnight, the whole town became poor. So that was the first thing that happened to us. All of a sudden we were all poor.

THE WAR STARTS (1939)

MANNIE: Anyway what had happened was this: Hitler tried desperately to provoke the Poles, in order to justify his war against Poland, so he could claim that the Polish people started the war instead of the Germans.

LEN: He faked that, didn't he?

MANNIE: Yes, that's exactly what he did. And what he did was this: In three places in Poland, a week before the war started, they took out criminals from the jails, who were under death sentence, and they put them in German uniforms. They sent them across the border, and they told them to shoot at Polish soldiers or border guards. If they managed to get away with it, they are pardoned, you know, from their death sentence. If not, they are going to die anyway. So, they might as well do a patriotic thing and serve the Germans' purposes. And our town was elected to be one of these three places.

And they sent over a German, in a German officer's uniform, with a machine gun, and somehow, a soldier noticed him coming across the border. And he yelled to him in Polish, "Stop!" And he yelled in German "Stop!" The guy didn't stop, so he shot him. So, of course, they brought the body to our home town. We didn't have cars so they brought him on a wagon, and the whole town was running after the wagon.

And some of the Poles, of course, they got very worked up about it, and they were yelling, "You Hitler, you," You this and you that, all kinds of names. And the what you would call the chief of police of our home town, was walking behind and did everything he could to keep them from abusing the body. That was Friday night. The war broke out a week later.

It turned out that the chief of the police was a German spy. When the Germans came in, the first thing they did is, because people used to loot places, to put in a sign on his home that nobody is allowed to get in. So, right away there was a sign, "This is forbidden territory." Loot your next door neighbor, but don't loot that fellow, you know.

Now, when the Germans came into our city, what happened was, they were looking for a priest, and they found him in a village, hidden. And that priest, exactly a week before the war broke out, took out some telecommunication equipment from the *Telegraphing*, the Polish telegraph agency, He took it to the border, and he delivered a speech to Hitler. And he said, "You Hitler, you want the Corridor?"

The Polish Corridor was a strip of land that gave the newly reconstituted state of Poland access to the Baltic Sea after World War I. The Corridor cut off East Prussia from the rest of Germany, and was bitterly resented by the Germans.

And he went on, "Sure, we'll give you the Corridor. But we'll also give you a broom to sweep it. The only thing we could give you," he said, "is, we got three and a half million Jews, you could take them all. All the Jews of Poland, you could have them for free. But otherwise, you won't get nothing [sic], you won't get a button off our shirt. That's it."

When the Germans came in, they went to look up that priest, you know, and they found him, and he was the first victim. They hung him and another Pole in the market place. The whole town had to go and look, and for three days, they didn't let them take it off. It was still warm, the body was decomposed, it started to smell, and on the top of it, they shot him through with machine guns. You could recognize nothing. It was just a skeleton here and there. The clothes were the only one that kept it together. And for three days, he was hanging there. He was the first one that got shot in town.

GOODS STOLEN AND RECOVERED

Soon after the Germans invaded Poland from the west, the Russians invaded from the east. When the two armies met it took the negotiators several weeks to fix the border. During that time, the Jews were moved from place to place.

MANNIE: We had a neighbor, a Pole. And my father went in to him and said, "Look, we have lived all our lives together. Our parents lived together. We know each other. We never had an argument. We always were peaceful neighbors. We are forced to leave home. I'll take all my furniture in to your house. If, God willing, we survive the war, we'll come back and we'll get it. And if *Chas v'cholila* [God forbid] not, we don't need it anyway. You might as well have it. Otherwise, somebody else will come and rob it anyway."

So, he [the neighbor] said, "Fine." And he was very touched by it, really, the old fellow. And he said, "You know what? I'll tell my son, Wednesday morning, and he'll take a couple of horses and put your other things in the wagon, and he'll take you to your destination." We had to go 40 kilometers because they had changed the Russian-German border.

We came to the town where we were supposed to go, and there was a bridge which the Germans had bombed. And the bridge was sort of... it wasn't really destroyed; with a wagon you still could go by it. So, it was passable. You see, the Germans had provided wagons for us, actually. The German sentry, he was standing by the bridge, told to the Polish drivers, "Look, fellows, if you want to go across, that's fine with me. But you won't come back because once you go across, you are in Russia."

So, when these Poles heard that they can't come back, they aren't going to take you across. You can't blame them for it. And they took us and threw off all our stuff. And instead of leaving, all of a sudden, every one of them had sacks prepared, and they started to rob us. Whatever they could, they packed into the sacks, and they ran away.

And here you see people, you know, in desperation, people were crying, people were fainting. They didn't know what to do with themselves. You were driven out of your home, and all of a sudden whatever you took with you, they robbed you again. There was no place to go. And some of them said they are not going anywhere. If they are supposed to die, they might as well die here. They are not going. They gave up.

I remember, just as now, a Jewish girl, her father was a butcher in town, and she said, "I don't care for my stuff. I don't care what you guys say. I'm going across and see what happens." She went across. She went straight to the German kommandantur, to the headquarters of the German army. And went in. And I don't know how she got in to the fellow in charge there, but she managed to get in, and told them what happened. She told them that the town people from our home town were driven out of town, and some people were supposed to take us across the river, and the sentries didn't let them, and they robbed us on the top of it, and they went home.

And that officer came out on a motorcycle by himself, and we all heard him scolding the sentry. "Who gave you permission to tell the Poles not to take us [sic] across the border?" Because the other town was really in German hands yet, so it was still German territory. And, anyway, he really was scolding him and yelling at him, and he went and brought a squad of motorcycles, army soldiers, Germans, with motorcycles, and it took about an hour, an hour and a half, and they brought all the wagons back, and made them give up all the stuff, back, that they robbed us. And told them to load it up, and take us across the border, and [several words inaudible] and then they'll go back.

LEN: That's a miracle!

MANNIE: That's a miracle. But what I'm trying to tell you, the boy came back, my next door neighbor, who drove us, you know, he came back and he started to load up again, and give us back the stuff that he robbed us. And I went to school with the guy. He used to come every Friday night to our home. I used to give him a piece of fish, with a piece of challah [Sabbath bread]. He used to love it. I used to go to his mother, and she used to give me food. She used to promise me that she won't tell my parents that I ate in her house, because it wasn't kosher.

We were really friends. In the small towns, we had to do fire watch. So every two houses, every night, they used to assign two houses, and he and I used to walk around at night, just in case a fire breaks out. So, I used to go with him every time, whole nights, you know. We were chums, good friends.

And I asked him, Vatsik was his name, and I said "Vatsik, I don't know what happened. I understand you didn't want to take us across the border when the sentry told you that you can't come back. This I could understand. But how in the world did you know to have sacks ready for the loot, to rob us? Was it premeditated? Did somebody tell you about it? Did you know ahead of time?"

You know, he got red in his face, like a beet, like a red beet, and he wouldn't answer. He wouldn't talk to me. So that was our first experience of our good neighbors. And the end was that this town remained with the Germans anyway.

ACROSS THE RIVER IN THE NICK OF TIME

After the invasion, the Germans moved the Jews from town to town. The following occurred in Ostrolenka.

MANNIE: And it was on a Sunday. Some Jews from our home town gave us a message. Two Germans are looking for us. And of course, father went in right away into a neighbor's house and he stayed there.

And finally, they found us. An officer came. He was a captain in the German army, and he was driven by a chauffeur in a motorcycle, a three-wheeler, you know. So, he told the chauffeur to stay down, and he'll go up and see the people.

And he was sort of rough, you know. We looked out the window, and we saw him coming. And he came up, and he was knocking on the door and yelling, "Open up, dirty Jews!" And we were really scared. My mother was so scared.

We let him in. He took off his raincoat and turned around to my mother and said in German, "Frau Berliner, don't you recognize me?" And right away, he told Mother his name, you know. And he was my father's partner. This man was inducted into the army, and he came to look us up. He was told that we were exiled from our home town.

And as soon as Mom found out who he was, she right away sent me next door to call Father, and then he [the Captain] told her the reason he was yelling downstairs, because he had to show the soldier. He didn't want to tell why he was "going to Israel," but he had told him it was something real important, and that why he was so rough. So, he was sorry if he scared us.

And anyway, he asked us whether we needed anything, whether we wanted anything, and he also told us, "Don't wait one day. Get away. Get away. Don't stay." And he told us that this city will be staying with the Germans. He said, "If you want to, I could get you an escort to take you out, but get away. Don't stay, because, sorry to tell you, there's no place for you."

I mean, you couldn't blame that German. He did it because all those years he was partners with my father. His kids might have been Nazis because they were indoctrinated in the schools, you know. But he had nothing to do with that. But anyway, we went around to tell people what happened, and there was another family, actually, from our home town, that was also partner with my father. And I don't know, but I believe he looked them up too. But those were days that you were always so busy with yourself, you know.

Anyway, we went across the river right away. A few hours later, at sunset, they closed the border.

EXPLAINING CAPITALISM TO A COMMUNIST OFFICIAL

The Russians moved the Berliner family to a lumber camp in Siberia, where Mannie became a lumberjack. On several occasions the head of the camp protected the workers from maltreatment.

MANNIE: This same official, the one that was a fine man, he used to love to sit with us. We never were afraid of him, you see. Like, we used to make a fire and sit. Don't forget, it was always cold there, so we had a fire, and we would sit and get warm, and we used to tell each other stories. We used to go in the morning to the restaurant — there was a restaurant where we used to go to eat breakfast before going to work — and we used to get a little bit of cereal and a little slice of bread.

And the bread we didn't eat. We used to take it in our pocket, and we used to have it for break time. Let's say at 10 o'clock we used to have a break time, and everybody used to pull out this piece of bread from the pocket and toast it on the fire. And everybody used to gloat over the piece of bread and tell how in his own town this big, famous bakery used to sell pastry, and this little bread represented the pastry he used to eat at home. And the boss used to laugh to hear the stories, that guy, you know.

And one day, I remember, it was one of our fellows who was from Warsaw. He was a big guy, a big-city fellow, and he tried to explain to that master how the capitalist system worked in Poland. And he told him, "Look, you need a pair of pants, and you go into the store. And you say you want a pair of pants. He wants 20 dollars for it. Now, if you go to the guy and tell him if he'll give you a good price, you might buy two pair, he would give you two for 18 dollars each. You go tell him that you need a dozen, he might give it to you wholesale for 15 dollars. If you are a very shrewd operator, you might come and say 'Hey, fellow, your people are going around without work anyway. What could you give me as an offer for a whole carload of pants?' You could get it for 10 dollars."

And you know, I'll never forget the look on the boss's face.

He jumped up and said, "Say, fellows, that's enough. That's a bunch of capitalist propaganda. How much is a pair of pants?" he says. "What do you mean? Every time you speak, it goes down in price. Haven't you got a price for a pair?" He wouldn't believe us, you know. He couldn't believe that if we buy two pair, it costs cheaper than one pair. Because in Russia there was no such thing. They don't sell you two pair. You only get one pair. And he wouldn't believe it.

SAVING A CHILD

Later, the Berliner family moved from Siberia to Turkestan. When the war ended, they were sent to a displaced persons camp in Stettin.

MANNIE: It happened to us, after the war of course, we tried to get as many Jews as we could out of Poland, but also, a main preoccupation with us was of getting out children who were saved by the Church or by Polish families who forcibly tried to baptize them when they were too young to know any different way. In most cases, it was infants, really, which parents literally threw over the fence, you know, on a yard with a home, that maybe they'll survive.

As a matter of fact, some of these children even knew their names. The parents wrote down the name, the name and the family, just in case the Poles would be willing after the war to return the child. But it turned out that in most cases we had to rescue it out of the Church because they wouldn't come forward and tell us who was left.

So, it was Poles, actually, who used to come and tell us how to find these children, the same Poles who during the war used to go and squeal to the Germans that there is a Jew hidden near and get a pound of salt for it. They would come to us and say that for so-and-so money, they will tell us where a Jewish child is.

But anyway, we gathered together some children, and we had lots of problems with them because they were fully indoctrinated with anti-Semitism. They were really brought up anti-Semites. They didn't want to be Jews, and they hated Jews, and they didn't want to have anything to do with us.

But, it happened in one case, where a woman brought to us — I think she was about 30 years old — a girl that she raised as her child. But this girl somehow, even though she must have been 5 or 6 years old anyway when she got here, somehow she couldn't remember a thing about the past. The earliest she could remember was when she was brought into this Polish family.

Until Friday night. In the camp we used to light candles, and this girl saw the candles, and she started to cry. We really couldn't stop her. She was crying and crying and crying, and all of a sudden she remembered. As a matter of fact she performed for us the ceremony — she showed us the way her mother used to do it. She told us exactly the way her mother used to put a kerchief on her head, and how she used to make the blessing. And she really performed for us the candle ceremony the way our mothers used to do. And she remembered her mother.

And all of a sudden, she said she'll stay with us. Now that she remembered, all of a sudden. And her foster mother was really happy about it because she felt that her place should really be with Jewish people.

The whole camp, you know, everybody was crying. She

kept us all in tears, for a whole week. But anyway, it turned out that we managed to save her. But, with most of these children that we saved, did we have trouble. Every time we used to go for a walk or something, as soon as we went by a church, they used to all run into the church, and they used to kneel and start to cross themselves, and yell, "I hate Jews. I don't want to be with the Jews!" All kinds of anti-Semitic slogans, you know, and we had a job to collect them again. Later, we got wiser. We used to send more people with them, so we could take better care of them. We had lots of trouble with them.

And that's another, actually, war crime: to take kids and forcibly convert them to Christianity.

NOTE: Mannes (Morris) Berliner was my first cousin, the oldest son of my father's sister Esther. He was born in Myszyniec, (pronounced "Mishinyetz") in northeastern Poland. He was 17 years old in 1939 when the Germans and Russians invaded Poland, starting World War II. After the war, he married Sonia Slutzky, whom he met in a displaced persons camp. They moved to Winnipeg, where she had relatives, and Mannes became a grocer. They had two daughters. Mannie died in 1999 at the age of 77.

SARAH CONNELLY'S energy and gentle humor have been a part of the class for many years, and she has spearheaded many of the projects and programs. She has assembled the large collection of stories written in class into books for our library and has been active in the production of the class's TV series shown on the Rossmoor channel. This story is an excerpt from a book she has worked on over the years about the internment of her family in a Japanese Camp in Baguio, Mountain Province, Luzon, Philippines.

WELCOME TO CAMP JOHN HAY

Rest stops along the way were few, and our burdens had become heavy. The group had been advised by the guards who accompanied us not to straggle and to try to keep up. The few Filipinos along the route watching us silently had been unable to help. At first it had seemed like a lark to us, but as the day had grown warmer and we had grown wearier, our parents started to hear complaints, and bundles had been lightened or switched. We were relieved when we finally arrived at our destination. Maybe now we could rest and have something to eat.

The kitchen crew had arrived much ahead of the rest of the group and had already set up a system to give us our first meal.

We were herded into the first of several barracks in Camp John Hay which had previously housed several hundred military men. Ours was a one-story affair, but most of the other buildings had two stories. The two-story building right next to us housed over a thousand Chinese families. They were three times as crowded as we were, but they did not stay there long. The Chinese prisoners were released, we thought, as soon as the Japanese felt they had conquered China. The consensus was that there were just too many Chinese for the Japanese to feed.

Initially, our family, my father and mother, my brother, my two sisters, and I, plus Bertram, a little Jewish boy, who had been boarding with us prior to the Japanese invasion, were housed together. But as soon as the Chinese families left, the men and older boys were moved to separate barracks, thus starting years of physical separation from their wives and families. Families with small children were placed in one area and single women and families with older kids in yet another.

Our new "quarters" consisted of one double-bed mattress and one twin mattress placed side by side on which the six of us slept. Soon, when some missionaries were released, Bertram was sent to his mother. I still don't know where they spent the years between 1941 and 1945.

The sleeping area was laid out like a big "O" with some sleeping around the perimeter and others with their mattresses spread out filling the center. The Japanese guards made incessant rounds of the "O" and we were watched constantly.

Though we kids were wary of the soldiers, we were not afraid of them and did not feel they were unfriendly. In fact, there were times when they played with and teased the children. They seemed to be especially fond of the babies, often taking a crying child out of its mother's arms to carry it and jiggle it to quiet its cries.

Every morning and every evening we were summoned for roll call. We were each given a number written on a piece of cloth which we pinned to our clothes. We kept the same number throughout our internment. For roll call, we formed groups of about 30 people. We had to stand at attention until the whole count was over. Whenever the Japanese had an important announcement to make, they had us line up the same way. We were also required to bow on command and say, "*Ohio guzaimous, hai tai san*," which meant, "Good morning, honorable soldier!"

After evening roll call, which generally took place on the adjacent tennis courts, the men and women were allowed to "commingle" with their families. The commingling was a promenade of women walking one direction in a circle and the men in a smaller circle walking in the other direction. That was not very satisfactory, so soon we were allowed to walk in the same direction as long as a certain distance was kept between the sexes. Guards watched constantly, but it didn't keep notes from being passed secretly on occasion or, once in awhile, a hand held. Children played in the center while parents visited, and I remember this as being a particularly beautiful time of the day. The sunsets in the Philippines are noted for their beauty, and the air was usually warm, so despite the war around us, the families were trying to make the best of the few moments they could share before we were again herded to our separate barracks. Always at the back of our minds and on the tips of our tongues was, "This won't go on too long — soon we'll be out and back home again."

Our camp was surrounded with barbed wire fences. At the front gate was a small house, probably the former office of the barracks commander. This was used by the Japanese as a guard house. The soldiers continually entered and left this building.

Camp John Hay had been the second target of Japanese bombs after Pearl Harbor. Just beyond the guardhouse, we could see huge craters in the once fine parade grounds — huge craters made by bombs that obliterated our water supply. (You must remember that what were "huge" to us children were probably merely pock marks to an adult.) Our camp had no running water. Imagine over 500 people and no running water! Emergency supplies for drinking were demanded and obtained, but there was no water to flush toilets with. Eventually, when we got a trickle of water, it was still in short supply. Then water was collected after kitchen vegetables were washed and used for skimpy baths and to flush the multiple, often filled toilets. The stench was horrible.

Crews were immediately formed to dig trenches behind the barracks for a multi-use outhouse. Makeshift divider curtains were hung. A fire-bucket holder was placed over the trenches to make a "six-holer." Flies were in abundance, and toilet paper, almost non-existent, was handed out by a monitor one piece at a time. (It came to pass in years to come that our toilet paper was 4x4 inch squares of newspapers and old magazines — still doled out one piece at a time.)

This was a community toilet not just for ladies or men. The hour was divided. The men would "go" during one half hour and the women the next. If you missed your half hour, you just had to wait. The showers were the same except that more time was allotted.

Dysentery started to become a problem along with the shortage of food and water. Concentrated efforts at cleanliness and sanitation were maintained, but it seemed like a downhill battle against the flies and disease.

*

Bong! Bong! Bong! Captain Kingcome strode down the aisle banging on a gong, the type used by mountain natives, the Igarotes, for their ceremonial dances. His booming voice announced, "Quiet hour!" Bong! "Quiet hour!"

Quiet hour came twice a day, and the gong was also sounded to announce roll calls and mealtimes. During the quiet hour, everyone was required to rest to conserve energy. Even if we didn't sleep, we had to be quiet. We never had enough food, and so the mandatory rest periods were strictly adhered to. I don't know if they were imposed by our own leaders or by the Japanese. Anything else of general interest was also announced by the booming voice of Captain Kingcome as he walked up one aisle and down the other.

Certain rituals had to be adhered to. The Japanese and our camp leaders insisted that the place be kept clean, so the bedding that was spread for sleeping was ritually rolled up each morning, and the floors were scrubbed every day. Daily menus, constantly changing camp rules, notices of lost and found, poems of encouragement, jokes or for sale items (some people were desperate for money and sold anything of value they still possessed), were posted by the front door, and this was a gathering spot to pick up the latest rumors and gossip.

Just before the war broke out, I had spent a weekend with friends and had picked up a persistent bladder infection. It had been weeks, and I was not getting better. My mother was worried. My Aunt Beulah, a doctor, advised that I be allowed to go "outside" with three other very sick people to get treatment at the Catholic hospital. Aunt Beulah would be able to make hospital calls to her patients and would see me every day. I was there about a week before the Japanese decided that we should all come back into camp. It seemed like a year. After all, I was only nine years old. The nuns were good to me, but I missed my family and friends.

&

This seems like a good time to tell you that besides the six in our immediate family, there were others from our extended family also interned. My dad's sister, Beulah, and her son were in our camp with us. Beulah's husband, Sam, had lost his life in the notorious Bataan Death March. In Santo Tomas Prison in Manila, my mother's sister, her husband and three children were incarcerated also.

&

Back at camp, life went on as usual. Kids of similar age and sex grouped together. We played endless games of "fish" and "Monopoly" and "spit." I learned to play jacks. We would sit out on the porch that almost surrounded the barracks and bounce that ball to get the first one, then two, and eventually all of the jacks. We told stories and gossiped.

"Mrs. D. and Mrs. McD. must be actresses. They always wear so much makeup." Each of these women had lost a leg and used crutches. They were immaculately groomed at all times, much to the amazement and admiration of the impressionable girls.

"Did you hear about the five men they took out to question? They are giving them the water treatment."

We were aware of the atrocities against men suspected by the Japanese of knowing military secrets. Some men never came back.

"I heard Mrs. B. is pregnant."

"How can she be? She is so skinny."

"She is skinny because she walks so fast."

Mrs. B. was pregnant. She took daily fast walks around and around the tennis courts. She lost the baby. It was buried in a shoe box, we heard. We all felt so sorry for her, and being kids, we thought that it was her walking fast that caused it. Don't ever think that women are the only gossips. We young girls did our share.

Our mattress lay at the end of the large open area of the barracks. (I remember before they moved the men and Bertram was still with us, how we used to take turns with the two of us sleeping at the bottom crosswise to everyone's feet!)

Beyond our allotted spot were small rooms, possibly pre-war housing for sergeants or battalion chiefs. Special people got to live in these rooms. The one just beyond our heads was the room occupied by the former lumber company boss who was chosen to be the civilian head of our camp, mostly because of his pre-war dealings with the Japanese. Mr. H.'s whole family, consisting of his wife, son and daughter, lived there. It also contained the office to which the Japanese guards constantly reported.

"Little Japanee girl, little Japanee girl," the Japanese guards would tease as they passed our quarters.

I had a haircut that was typical of the little Japanese girls

— sometimes called a Dutch boy bob. They knew they got my goat because I dived under the pillow each time they said it.

Another room housed an elderly doctor, retired, and his tall, slender, red-headed wife. The red hair was another topic of children's gossip. My aunt, the doctor, and her infant son also lived in this room.

Every time we partook of our meals at our bed and Mr. H. would pass, he, too, would tease, "What? Eating again?" His teasing would anger me.

Hungry tongues wag with rumors. Several people believed that because these particular people were the camp leaders they always had extra food in their quarters. Many were constantly suspicious and jealous. This is a normal feeling in this type of situation. It always seems like someone has more than you do when you have nothing. This experience helped me in later life to better understand those suffering from poverty and hunger.

*

Some other girls, organized by a particularly talented teenager, prepared a program to be presented during one of the evenings the Japanese allowed us entertainment. It was a depiction of life in camp acted by the teenage girls and boys portraying dominant characters in the camp. It was a musical, and the lyrics of certain popular songs of the late 30s and early 40s were changed to suit the situation. A former science teacher helped with the lyrics, and everyone pitched in to make the production a success. Stage materials were non-existent so improvisation was imaginative. The stage was made up of several long tables pushed together. There was an abundance of talent in the camp as people came from every walk of life: missionaries, business people, miners, school teachers, lumbermen, British refugees from China, etc.

The only song I remember is, "There's a great day coming mañana, with a wonderful, wonderful dream… We'll be out of the doldrums, mañana…"

Oh, didn't we dream of beer and pretzels though? That's all we ever dreamed of or talked about — FOOD — that and the rumors of what was happening on the outside. Our diet of rice for every meal, soft, mushy rice for breakfast and either fried, soft, mushy rice or regular boiled rice for dinner, was not too inspiring. Our meals at this time were supplemented with a few home grown beans and vegetables, and bits and pieces of food that were brought into camp in cans or sent in by loyal Filipinos. This is why people sold their belongings. They needed money to supplement their larder. Milk was saved for the babies, and the workers got slightly larger portions. There was always the persistent rumor that the kitchen people got all they could eat, and it did seem some people never did lose any weight. We had two regular meals and, while it lasted, a mid-afternoon snack those first few months. A cry heard more often than one would like was, "I'm hungry, Mom."

Nothing was thrown out. Parts of vegetables that ordinarily would have been thrown out were cooked and served and eaten. The water they were cooked in was saved for soup. The crust that is formed on the pan when rice is cooked was removed and served. As the years went on, the quality of food deteriorated. Weevils and worms came with the rice and beans. Women were organized to sort out as many impurities from the raw food as they could, the rocks which were put in the rice to make it weigh more, plus worms and weevils. However, they couldn't get them all, and we did consume our share.

From the beginning, however, from child to oldest adult, we were always optimistic that tomorrow the war would be over, and we would see a triumphant American army march in and take us away. Maybe it was because I was a child that tomorrow was the next day and not just a future possibility.

NOTE: After nearly four years of incarceration 12-year-old Sarah and her family were repatriated by the American Army in May of 1945. They moved to California, living with relatives for a time. Married, with a family, and after fifty years in the same house, Sarah recently moved to New Mexico. She's the treasurer of Bay Area Civilian Ex-Prisoners of War, which is affiliated with American Ex-POWS. Attending one of their reunions was their former Japanese commandant. Although the group's focus is education of the thousands of civilians held prisoners in the Far East Theater, Sarah would prefer to "downplay the past and concentrate on getting the world to learn to love each other and get along despite our differences."

1945, Manila, the Philippines — American children atop a tank after being freed from their Japanese internment.

Photo courtesy National World War II Museum, New Orleans, Louisiana

HELEN KNOPP, a stately, gracious woman with a beautiful smile, paints a picture with words using the same creativeness she employs with her artwork. For several years she treated the group to readings on her close-knit German family's history in Oakland, California in the 1900's. No longer able to attend class on a regular basis or read aloud herself — but continuing to enthusiastically write — she has relied on our facilitator, Mary Webb, to read her work aloud and solicit critiques.

EXCLUSION ORDER #19

This memorable incident took place at the end of April, 1942, about five months after the United States became involved in World War II. I had already earned my secondary teaching credential and was studying for my Master's Degree in German and working as a teaching assistant in the German Department of the University of California in Berkeley.

All of us teaching assistants shared an office in room 404 of Wheeler Hall. From our window there we had become used to seeing and hearing units of the ROTC (Reserve Officer's Training Corps) drilling on the campus in their uniforms. We were aware that knowledge of the languages of our enemies was vital to the military forces. This need contributed to the growth of the German Department.

In other respects, however, since students were still being allowed to complete their immediate educational goals before being drafted, the campus seemed like an oasis, largely unaffected by the war. We in room 404 were a studious but carefree lot.

On this particular day, April 30, 1942, a Thursday, there was a near capacity crowd of teaching assistants filling the room. All the chairs were occupied; two or three people sat on every desk; and someone even sat at one end of the broad window sill. The noon hour was well along, and the place was not only filled with cigarette smoke but was also buzzing with several simultaneous conversations.

It was at this point that the door suddenly opened and another of our group burst into the room. It was Betty Ito, whom we hadn't seen for over a week. As she moved across the room with quick, purposeful steps, boosted herself to a seat at the other end of the window sill, and faced us, all conversation stopped.

Several of us spoke at once.

"We've missed you."

"Where have you been?"

"That's what I've come to tell you," Betty replied. "Where I've been… and where I'm going!"

"Going? What do you mean, Betty?" we asked in disbelief.

"I'm going back home to Chicago where I can live with my family. And I've come to say goodbye. I'm leaving tomorrow morning."

"But why Betty? Why so suddenly? Why now, in the middle of the semester when you're so close to finishing your doctorate?" We were all looking for answers.

"Don't you read the *Berkeley Gazette*?" Betty demanded.

To be sure, I, from Oakland, did not. Others said they did occasionally, if they had time, but they hadn't noticed anything relevant.

"Oh my, then you don't know! You have no idea what a frantic time this has been for me! Well, the thing is that on April 21, the army issued Exclusion Order #19 calling for the evacuation from Berkeley of everyone of Japanese ancestry by noon on Friday, May 1! That's tomorrow! Anyone who hasn't left for someplace outside of California by then will be bussed to temporary quarters in a so-called 'assembly center' at the Tanforan Race Track in San Bruno. Then later they'll be taken to some unknown out-of-the-way inland internment camp. So you can see why I'm rushing to leave here before noon tomorrow."

"Oh, Betty, how awful! But why you? You're not an enemy! You're a citizen! You were born in Chicago!" We all spoke at once.

"With a name like Ito and my appearance, I obviously can't deny my ancestry, and the army seems to consider all of us dangerous!" A slight frown had formed on Betty's pretty, usually placid face, but it quickly disappeared as she went on, "But I consider myself really lucky! I have a place to go! And I can take all my things, not just as much as I can carry, like the other poor souls."

"But what about your Ph.D.? You're so close to getting it."

"Oh, that's where I've been lucky, too. It's such a fortunate coincidence that Professor Taylor was at the University of Chicago for more than twenty-five years just before coming here. He has been so helpful. He's been on the telephone day after day with people he knows there and with the administration here making all kinds of arrangements so

I'm going to be able to pick up in Chicago exactly where I'm leaving off here at U.C.!"

"That's great, Betty. But what about the class you teach?"

"Professor Taylor managed to have one of the professors take it over right away. I'm so thankful. I've had so much else to do! I've had to rearrange my whole life in ten days!

"First off I had to get my train ticket, no easy matter these days, so that on the day I was required to register at the Civil Control Station down on Channing Way, I could convince them I was going to Chicago and didn't need to go to Tanforan.

"There have been so many loose ends to take care of. I've been on the phone and running hither and yon all these days, meanwhile packing up all my belongings. Just this morning all my boxes were picked up for shipment to Chicago. That was such a relief! So now I could finally find the time to come to see you and say goodbye."

"We hate to see you go, Betty. We'll miss you!"

"I'll miss you people, too. You've been great friends, and I wish I didn't have to leave."

Betty paused and looked down, probably trying to control her emotions. Then suddenly she jumped down from her perch on the window sill, saying, "I've got to go now. I still have lots to do. I'm glad so many of you were here today. Please tell the others."

While she spoke, Betty crossed the room and opened the door. Then she turned and said with feeling, "I love you all. Please remember that and take care!" With those words she quickly turned again and left.

"Same to you, Betty! And best wishes!" we called after her as the door closed.

For the next minute we all sat in stunned silence. My eyes were moist. Probably others were, too. Some folks sat shaking their heads; some stared at the floor. The smokers, having forgotten to smoke during Betty's visit, now shook the long ash ends from their cigarettes and ground the butts into their ash trays with uncommon fierceness.

Through our open window came the familiar sound of marching feet and the harsh commands of a drill sergeant, but now, with Betty Ito's visit, the war had definitely touched our campus oasis.

On my long streetcar ride home that afternoon, my mind churned with all that Betty had told us and with thought of the implications of this evacuation. At the dinner table I eagerly told my family the whole story of Betty's upsetting experience. At the end I turned to Father with some questions.

"How come we didn't know this was happening— right here in Berkeley? You did read to us a month or more ago about the removal of the Japanese from some island up in Washington and from an area around San Pedro and Long Beach, then soon after that from parts of San Francisco along the ocean front and around the Golden Gate. Just the other night you told us about the F.B.I. rounding up Japanese aliens in Berkeley. But, Papa, did you see anything in our newspapers about this total Japanese evacuation from Berkeley— including American citizens?"

"Actually, yes, and there have been other places, too, but if I didn't mention it, it was because of other important news. Now, however, there is a front-page article in this evening's paper that I was definitely going to call to the family's attention the first thing. It involves Oakland."

"Oh, my goodness! Oakland, too?" I exclaimed!

Referring now to the *Oakland Tribune* that lay next to his place at the table, Father went on, "This article tells about Exclusion Orders Nos. 27 and 28. Number 28 calls for 'complete evacuation of Japanese from the cities of Oakland, Emeryville, Alameda and Piedmont.' It goes on to say, 'Bay Farm Island, thickly populated by Japanese, must also be cleared.' It says they must all be evacuated by noon on May 7."

"Why that's just one week from today!" my brother Harold exclaimed.

"Alameda? Bay Farm Island? Oh, dear. That's where Fugi and his family lives!" Mother said thoughtfully with a look of concern.

Just then the telephone rang, and Mother, who received most of the calls in our family, hurried to the front of the house to answer. While she was gone, the rest of us spoke about Fugi and how this would affect him.

Fugi, our capable Japanese gardener, had been coming to us faithfully whenever needed for a number of years. He worked so quickly and efficiently, was always so willing to do anything we asked and then did it better than we expected, that we enjoyed having him more and more frequently. He obviously loved the soil and all growing things. Often I saw him down on his knees smoothing the top soil with his hard-working bare hands and making newly placed plants look right at home. At other times I admired his agility as he stood on a ladder and with a quick and practiced eye, spotted the branches to trim on our fruit trees.

We had never asked Fugi his age. By the way he worked, we would never have guessed he was a grandfather, but he often spoke proudly of his two grown sons and their young children. It was obvious from what he told us that he dearly loved his hard working wife of many years, and their home and family. And we had grown to love him.

Mother came rushing back from the telephone, her face filled with anguish. She seemed to be on the point of crying.

"That was Fugi on the phone!" she said. "He is indeed caught up in this evacuation, and he called to tell me— just imagine, that dear man apologized when he told me— that he wouldn't be able to come tomorrow as he had promised. He and his wife have too much to do. They have only seven days, mind you, seven days, to make all the arrangements for leaving home. That includes selling their house and all their possessions, or trying to, for, what with all the other Japanese trying to do the same, they may, in the end, have to give everything away.

"And all this goes for his two sons and their families, too. They have their homes and even a nursery they'll need to dispose of. And none of them has any place to go, as Betty Ito does, so they'll have to be bussed off to Tanforan and to no telling where else, taking only what basic necessities they can carry!

"Oh, why should these good-hearted, honest, hardworking, family people have to go through all this? And Fugi and his wife already grandparents! And the grandchildren, still so young and innocent. What harm could any of them do? I wonder what lies ahead for these dear people."

And now, over sixty years later, as I write of that day, I am still left wondering. Although Fugi promised to keep in touch if he could, we never heard from him or his family again.

NOTE: Helen left U.C. but remained loyal, forming an endowment there with her brother for the library and scholarships. She became office manager and VP of Knopp Inc., an electrical testing equipment company founded by her father in 1928. During the war it made products for the armed services. She remained there for 35 years but continued her teaching of German part time at College of the Holy Names in Oakland, California. After retirement she began writing — with the group's encouragement — her family's long history in Oakland, weaving local and national events into intimate family scenes. (In '42) "I watched a whole Japanese community in Oakland fold," she commented. "I was sorry at the time and sorry now."

From National Archives & Records Administration (NARA), College Park, MD.
1942 — Tanforan Racetrack in San Bruno, California where Japanese Americans reported for internment by the United States government.

JOHN CLINE was the most prolific author of the Rossmoor Writers. He read his work — most often autobiography and poetry — with the resonant voice of a corporate attorney, his profession of many decades. John died in 2003 at age 83, leaving a major void in the group. But he left us thousands of his words, including the following selection, written while traveling with friends: his reaction to visiting the Babi Yar Monument in Ukraine.

A DAY OF SORROW AND GRIEF

Last night I re-read *Babi Yar* by Yevtushenko. Some of the words repeat themselves as I rush through lunch:

The wild grasses rustle over Babi Yar
The trees look ominous
like judges.
Here all things scream silently,
and, baring my head,
slowly I feel myself
turning gray.
And I myself
am one massive, soundless scream
above the thousand thousand buried here.
I am
each old man
here shot dead.
I am
every child
here shot dead.
Nothing in me
shall ever forget!"

Today Marvin and Barbara Parsons and I take a cab to Babi Yar for the bargain price of three packs of cigarettes. The ride is a short five minutes from the center of Kiev. Weather is dressed gloriously bright today. The sun dances on the changing fall colors in the leaves— those which remain attached to the trees and those departed. The air is still but blows crisp through the rolled down taxi window on the driver's side. The taxi scatters leaves and creates a stream of them that flutter high, settle quietly behind as we pass.

The post-board in front of the Babi Yar monument reads in Ukranian:

Dorogi Street!
Arise people of the world!
29 September
A day of sorrow and grief
29-9-1941 Babi yo yar

When my eyes read this last line, I re-read it. The impact is sudden and hard. Forty-nine years ago today! The slaughter began! The three of us are silent, held in place by some power. The history of these events pours through me.

The order read, "All Jews of the city of Kiev and its environs must appear on the corner of Melnik and Kokhtu Streets (beside the cemetery) at 8 a.m. on September 29, 1941."

Only moments ago the taxi passed the cemetery. This is Dokhtu Rov Street. Babi Yar is not outside Kiev, Babi Yar is *in* Kiev.

I see them now: the old, infirm and crippled men, the women, the children trudging with their small bundles, all that remains of what little they have. They enter the long passage formed by the files of soldiers and dogs. The corridor is narrow, only about five feet wide. The soldiers stand shoulder to shoulder, their sleeves rolled up. All are armed with rubber truncheons and big sticks.

They rain blows upon the people that run this gauntlet. It is impossible to hide, impossible to dodge. Blows draw blood at once, descend on heads, shoulders and back from right to left. "*Schnell! Schnell!*" shout the soldiers, laughing heartily, obviously enjoying themselves and trying to hit harder at sensitive places.

With each blow a person cries out; the women scream. People fall. The dogs are set upon them at once. One man gets up. Others remain where they lay. The crowd presses over them, treading on bodies, stamping them into the earth.

The maddened people emerge into a space cordoned off by the troops. This is a level grass field, littered everywhere with underwear, shoes and clothing. The Ukrainian Polizei seize the people, beat them and shout, "Undress! Quick! Quick!" Those who hesitate or move too slowly are forcibly stripped, kicked, beaten with brass knuckles and clubs. Many are streaked with blood.

The naked are lined up in small groups and led toward a narrow passage in a high earth wall. Mothers cling to children. Now and then a German or a Polizei loses his temper, snatches a child from its mother, strides to the earth wall, swings it in the air and hurls it over the top like a log of wood.

It grows dark.

Once through the passage, they emerge on the brow of a deep sand quarry with almost sheer walls. All are herded to the left, single file, along a very narrow ledge. The walls rise to the left. The quarry falls away on the right. The ledge, cut especially for the executions, is so narrow the people instinctively lean against the sand wall so as not to fall. The quarry is deep.

Below lay a sea of bloody bodies. Machine guns are strung out on the opposite side of the quarry, each manned by a German soldier. A camp fire behind silhouettes them clearly and casts their shadows on the dead below.

When the file of people fills the ledge, a German moves away from the fire, takes his place at his machine gun, barks an order and shoots. The bodies fall as the lines of fire reach them.

From the quarry bottom, muffled sounds of those that still live rise from the mass of bodies perceptively stirring. They settle deeper and tighter through the motions of those being buried alive.

Soldiers emerge on the brow of the quarry, and sweep the pits with their flashlights. Those who seem to be alive are shot with revolvers. Other soldiers, wading through the corpses, bend over and take things from them. Shoot at whatever moves.

Within minutes a voice shouts, "Come on, shovel away." The shovels create another sound as they cut into the sand followed by a thud as the sand crashes on the bodies. The men stop shoveling, satisfied that only a thin layer of sand is enough to suppress the stench.

More people are lined up on the ledge. In the nearby level grass-covered field, the Germans are sorting and stacking the clothing. Dogs fidget on their leashes. Horse-drawn carts come for the clothing.

Marvin and Barbara move. Their shadows cross mine. I return to September 29, 1990.

The silence cradles us. We walk with muted footsteps toward the sculptured Babi Yar Monument of the men, women, children rising from the pit. They face us as we approach. Some among them lift and strain to push children into the sky. The monument has replaced the machine guns.

The edge of the ravine cuts my vision as it drops sharply into the hollow, once the grave of 100,000 people, 50,000 of whom were murdered in the first five days. On the opposite bank, the cliff, the ledge. From here they fell. Today grass grows in the bowels of this abyss. Back from the opposite bank, trees bring their shadows to the edge and lean into the crater, a blanket softer than the harsh sand. My eyes follow the slope of the ravine into shadows too dark for me to see.

At the base of the monument is this message:

1941 – 1943
German Fascist troops shot 100,000 civilians and soldiers

It is written in Yiddish, Ukranian, and Russian.

The cab driver is waiting for us when we return. He had been instructed to wait and take us back to the hotel. We do not talk.

Among us there is a silence that speaks of loneliness, an emanation that rises from the simplicity of its utterance. Whatever its origin, it lingers, creates anew another silence as quiet as the one departing. There is a soundless echo, an echo that does not return, remains in the emptiness. In the front seat of the cab, my solitude dictates these lines:

> *Leaves are weeping.*
> *The grass is quiet.*
> *Wind speaks through tears.*
> *A harsh voice chokes humans*
> *into silence.*
> *Out of this hollow*
> *their spirits rise*
> *as they fall into forever.*
> *Wings of faith*
> *do not stop the thunder*
> *that engulfs them.*
> *They sink into the gulf*
> *of a storm through which*
> *they do not find a harbor.*

NOTE: *John was raised by an aunt and uncle in Brawley, a rough, California ranch town, yet spent his youthful summers in the elite, affluent beach town of La Jolla. He chronicled both. His impressions, written most often through dialogue, of coming of age in these diverse towns during the 1930s were donated to the La Jolla Library prior to his death. He was an ardent world traveler and reader, with thousands of books in his private library. Classmates benefited hugely from his keen listening ability; he took copious notes of each person's reading, then delivered a thoughtful, introspective critique loaded with positives. The Holocaust was one of his lifelong interests.*

Permission to print a segment of the poem Babi Yar *by Yevgeny Yevtushenko was granted by St. Martin's Press.*

LEO BACH'S eyesight may be dimming a bit but his wit at near ninety is still as sharp as ever. These stories are excerpts selected from his published war biography, Going Home. *It took years for Leo to write down what life in a POW camp was like for an American bombardier who also happened to be Jewish. Sometimes, when reading a chapter over the years, he would have to stop for a moment. His usually commanding voice would falter, but he would clear his throat and his voice would then demand your attention.*

EXCERPTS FROM
GOING HOME

THE STORY BEGINS:
JUMP!

"**P**ut your chute on and get the hell out of here! We're going down!" Blanche, the gunner, was out of the belly gunner's bubble before the pilot finished the sentence. Swearing, as only Bernie could, he snapped on his chute and jumped out. I could hear his words, "Son of a bitch." His words faded as he fell. He was out and drifting downward. That was the last time I saw Bernie Blanche. He made it all right, but I lost touch with him… forever.

My rush to become a prisoner of war started at three minutes after noon on April 11, 1944. As I floated down in my parachute, I remember looking at my watch, then looking up at my comrades rushing toward the target of the day. God, how quiet it was. I was alone, just a dot in the sky, drifting down to...? And here my story of being a POW begins.

CAPTURED, APRIL 13, 1944

I could see that I was going to hit the ground amid some young pine trees. That's good, I thought. Should I get entangled in a tree, my feet would probably hit the ground anyway. The trees were too small to do me any harm. As it turned out, the trees were not my problem. The rate of descent and the position of my body were such that I hit the ground completely off balance. The wind and swing of the parachute caused me to land on my right foot and my leg buckled. I could feel a shooting pain all up and down my right side. Damn, had I broken something? I didn't think so. After a brief examination and rubbing my leg, my guess was that I had gotten banged up and bruised, but not any broken bones. A good diagnosis as it turned out.

After breaking loose from my chute, I was able to move about on my leg, limping to be sure, but hey, a good adrenaline rush will overcome a lot of pain.

I had to do something with my parachute. Since I had neither the time nor the wherewithal to bury it, I did the next best thing. I covered it up with fallen branches from the young pine trees and moved away from it. By this time the pain in my leg had grown. I was hurting so I curled up under one of the pines. I lay curled around the two-inch tree trunk with the lower branches effectively covering me from view.

§🐝

The road curved slightly and coming around the curve I saw a woman on a bicycle approaching me. I did the only thing I could under the circumstances: I held up one hand with my other hand outstretched to show that I meant her no harm. I stopped. So did she. She turned slowly in her seat and held up her hand to signal another bicyclist to stop. I looked to where she was signaling and saw a young girl stop. Both stared in horror at the apparition before them and pointed over my shoulder. I turned and froze! There, not more than two feet away, stood a German soldier, his rifle raised and aimed at my head.

STALAG LUFT ONE –1944

"Lt. Bach, what's your outfit?" At first I couldn't hear what Capt. Smith, the Block Captain, was saying because the others in the room were pounding on the floor with broom handles, chairs, tin cans, shoes. They used whatever they could to make noise, which in effect would make it impossible to be overheard by the *ferrets* (a name we gave to the Germans who crawled underneath our barracks to spy on us and look for tunnels). We were always concerned about German infiltrators within the POW population. To that end newcomers were always interrogated by the Americans so I learned that my rather terse introduction was the norm.

The buildings were mostly built on two-foot stilts which provided the *ferrets* the crawl space they needed to do their spying. Their activities were usually confined to the hours after lockdown, when the guards would roam the compound with their dogs. Occasionally one guard would slip under the barracks to see and hear what he could.

Captain Smith continued, "What's your outfit, Lieutenant?"

"381st Bomb Group, Sir."

"What Squadron?

"534th, Sir."

"What was your tail insignia?"

"Triangle L, Sir."

"You can knock off the sir, Lieutenant."

"Thank you, Sir, er, ahh, I mean… "

"That's OK. What's your first name?"

"Leo, Sir… er, ahh… damn, Sir."

"You're not too smart, are you Leo?"

"No, Sir, I mean… Yes, Sir, I mean… oh shit… Sir, Captain, Sir… I don't know what I mean, Sir."

Captain Smith smiled and said, "You can call me Snuffy, Leo. OK? Now, where were you stationed?"

"Ridgewell, Sir, ahh… I mean Snuffy. Ridgewell."

"Station number?"

"167"

"Now you're getting it, Leo." Captain Smith turned to one of the men who was pounding on the floor, "Hey, Jimbo, go through the rooms and find out if anybody was in Triangle L, OK?"

"On my way, Snuffy, anything else?"

"No, I don't want to burden that peanut brain of yours. Now move your ass. Go!"

Block Ten yielded no one from Triangle L although there were some who knew the 381st Bomb Group, who knew that the 534th Bomb Squadron, Triangle L, was quartered in Ridgewell. This took some of the heat off, but it was by no means an automatic acceptance into the block. More had to be learned about me. I was told not to take it personally and was assured that once I was accepted I would see the wisdom of these precautions. Even if I didn't appreciate them at the time!

So as not to break my spirit entirely, I was told that until rooms were rearranged and space became available I would have to make the best of it sleeping in the hall. As long as I had *command* of the hallway, I was given the task of alerting the barracks of the approach of German guards. The signal was very straightforward, "Goon up!" It was picked up by any Kriegie (abbreviation of *kriegsgefangenen* — prisoner of war) who heard it and repeated it. Soon it became a loud cacophony of "Goon up." There was no way that anyone in the Block was not aware of the presence of Germans in the area. This gave us time to *get clean* if we were engaged in activities that were *verboten*.

Simple, but effective. So effective that even the German guards picked up on it and said it themselves as they entered the barracks. It was comical to hear the Germans alerting us to their own presence. "Goon up," coming from the mouths of the Germans, was a constant source of amusement. Even the Germans saw the humor.

It took about a week for the three of us newcomers to be cleared.

"Lt. Bach… Leo, why don't you collect your gear and come on in?"

I was lying on my bunk, outside of the door of room 7, when Lt. Dorseman uttered those simple but momentous words, "Come on in." I was almost a whole person again.

"Yes, sir!" I leaped from the sack, collected my scant

belongings and was through the door immediately, almost knocking Abe Dorseman ass over end.

"Damn it, Bach, you almost put tracks on my back, what's your hurry?"

"The hurry is, Lieutenant, I was afraid you would change your mind. You don't know how it feels out there in the hall."

"The hell I don't, Leo! Listen, I don't want you to get the idea that we were treating you any different than anyone else who came to us. They had to find out about me just as they had to find out about you, and you will put the next Kriegie through the same routine. It's the only way I know of to minimize the danger of the Gerries planting a ringer on us. How would you do it?"

I had no answer, so I just shrugged my shoulders. Dorseman went on, "Think of the poor bastards who got shot down that we couldn't verify for one reason or another. Think of how they felt. They are with us, but I imagine they feel less than good about their circumstance. Gradually they are brought into the fold, but I'm sure it must be a stinkin' situation while it lasts.

"What generally happens is that the Gerries pull out the infiltrators before it goes on too long. They are probably shipped to another compound to try to infiltrate there. Are they ever successful? Who knows? We can't ever be sure. Even about our own situation here. We have to assume they are as clever as we think we are. They play the same games we do. Just as we try to keep them occupied by our constant escape attempts, I'm sure they are working us over by keeping us busy checking them out. The Germans learn things from this process.

"The Germans would hear things. What group were you in? What tail letters for your group? Who was the C.O.? Things we would never tell them during interrogation. Remember: Name, Rank and Serial Number. Here could be the information they wanted, handed to them as a gift. This in effect keeps us from other mischief, which they can't control or are not aware of. Listen, they are just as smart as we are. The difference is that they have more resources at their disposal at the moment. Kapish?"

My only response was a nod of my head, accompanied by a sheepish grin.

One look around our room of fourteen men, called number seven, block ten, and it would be hard to imagine fits of loneliness. There wasn't a moment when you could be alone. A solitary walk around the compound was the only way to be alone with your thoughts.

At night, when the room was dark and the men were in their bunks, the room was relatively quiet. My thoughts turned to home and loved ones. Sometimes I could hear sobbing from one of the men. We made it a point not to try to identify the one in distress. We all had those very same feelings, and every once in a while it was another's turn to sob.

Seven double-decked bunks spread around a room no more than 15 feet by 20 feet didn't leave much room for dancing! Most rooms were pretty much like ours. Some had twelve men, some sixteen. The rooms were similar in size and arrangement. The determining factor was the capriciousness of the German Interior Decorators. This number was the way the Germans wanted it. Don't ask me why. They didn't allow us to rearrange the bunks. The Germans had a diagram of each room showing the position of the men in each room. They liked to think they knew where each Kriegie lived and slept. Whenever possible, we arranged moves from one room to another if there was good reason. Friendships were important for the Kriegies' well-being. For some guys it didn't matter. They kept pretty much to themselves. Others were more gregarious and more adventurous. Some slept in one room and hung out in another. Freedom! Oh freedom! Americans, what can you expect?

When it came to food… the thought was always gnawing at our stomachs, if such a thing is possible… almost as often as the thought of GOING HOME, which was always foremost on our minds.

One would think that with such a preoccupation it made Kriegies a rather self-centered group of men. Nothing could be further from the truth. It was precisely because of such universally held needs, that we became a most focused contingent of young men.

We were young men who, until recently, had been civilians. We had undergone a highly technical regimen of training along with a smattering of military training. Couple this with intelligent leadership in the persons of our C.O.s and we became a ragtag group of soldiers who developed an inner discipline. True, we were temporarily detained by the enemy, but our morale was bolstered by the belief that it was indeed temporary. This is not to say that we were oblivious to our circumstances!

Being a POW did not contribute to my well-being. There was loss of life. There was mental and physical assault, which took their toll. In spite of this, there developed camaraderie. It grew out of adversity; that made for good soldiers.

Good soldiers or no, we had to eat. We've all heard the adage, "An army travels on its stomach." While our travel plans were severely inhibited, we were still an army, after a fashion, and food was an integral part of our well-being. The lack thereof was always noted. If we had relied on German rations, it's safe to say many of us would not have made it. The Red Cross parcels saved our lives, but they were not always forthcoming. Whenever our Commanding Officers approached the Germans about our parcels, the answers were always the same, "*Your planes have bombed our trains and your parcels are lost.*" For a short period of time we got a parcel once a week. That didn't last long. Weeks at a time went by with nothing. No parcels at all! There were times when we would have to share parcels with one another. One parcel for two men. We knew in our hearts that Jerry was lying. They were stealing our food! Poor bastards were as hungry as we were. Supermen, my ass!

The Geneva Convention specifies that POWs were to receive rations "equivalent to the rations received by soldiers of the detaining power." I don't think they meant for us to share *our* food with the Germans. We found warehouses full of Red Cross parcels when we were liberated by the Russians. So much for the cock and bull stories about German trains being strafed by the 8th Air Corps. Oh, I'm sure our guys loved to hit the trains. That was a supply line that needed to be cut and cut them they did. It was evident by the tons of parcels that we found after liberation that trains did get through with our food, but as I said, the Germans were stealing and eating our food.

The rations supplied by the Germans were barely fit for human consumption. It is a testament to the intestinal fortitude of POWs, when faced with real hunger, what they will consume. On those days when they did supply a hot meal, it was a tub of hot water laced with cabbage and rotten potatoes and rutabagas and some grass. On very special occasions, there were pieces of horse meat. Special occasions, I suppose, were when a horse died. In each block there were approximately 200 men. Can you see a problem in the making here? How to ladle out the soup so that it at least had the appearance of being equal? An empty tin from a can of powdered milk — *KLIM was actually the name on the can* — was used as a measuring utensil. "X" number of cans full per room depending on the number of men in the room.

Then came the *Kriegsbrot*. This was a German concoction of sawdust, ground acorns, and I suppose some flour, which was baked into a loaf of bread. One loaf for seven men. In our room, with fourteen men, the two loaves had to be divided into sevenths. This task was assigned to one man with a steady hand and a sharp knife. End pieces caused a problem. The Germans frowned on the possession of sharp knives, but we managed to hone a sharp edge on some knives. They were kept out of sight, and occasionally they were confiscated by the Germans. Not too often, however. They were usually looking for other contraband, such as digging tools and shovels. They should have realized, after they did find some shovels that we carved from slats of wood that a sharp knife had to come into play. To my knowledge, they never did make the connection.

We collectively decided that each man would keep his own bread ration. The thinking was that some of us could go for a longer time between meals. Those who absolutely couldn't wait could nibble on a piece of bread as a pacifier. When the meal called for a sandwich each man had to supply his own bread.

There were times when the sandwich was without bread because a Kriegie used up his seventh of a loaf. We didn't like to part with what we had claimed, and it was not acceptable to borrow food.

Usually, with careful slicing, a Kriegie could yield eight or nine slices from his ration of bread. It took a sharp knife and a steady hand. Some men were very accomplished and would cut slices for others. It was not unusual to see some slices crumble. No matter. The sandwich might not look tidy, but it was food. The makings varied. A thin slice of Spam was a treat. Whenever a Canadian Red Cross parcel made its way into the camp it was a very special treat. The Canadian parcels had a tin of Argentinean beef and a tin of real butter. That was a time when our sandwiches received special attention and each bite was savored.

There were more times than I care to remember when pickings were slim. A sandwich was nothing more than a spread of margarine. Margarine in those days was not as good as it is today. I remember some that had a little envelope of coloring to add to the margarine to make it look like butter. Cudahy's — that was it!

All rations other than bread were donated to the larder and our cooks for the day performed their magic. We assigned the jobs on a rotating basis, usually a week at a time. Lunch and dinner were a collective endeavor. Breakfast was left to the individual to make his own tea or coffee with a piece of bread. Usually those pieces that crumbled were reserved for breakfast. Sorry sir, no OJ...

ONE MEMORABLE DAY...

An incident occurred that was forever branded in my mind. I wish I could forget, but the image just won't go away. In the total scheme of things it wasn't a terribly big deal, but it bothered the hell out of me.

There was a flurry of activity throughout the prison grounds. All the old men and misfits were left to guard us. That wasn't entirely true; they filled in whenever there was a need. The regulars still ran the show. I'm sure the old men resented being thrown together with the misfits. Activity such as this usually meant visiting brass. This was the case that day.

Three large limousines stopped in front of the gate. Men in long black leather greatcoats poured from the limousines. Their felt hats were pulled straight down to their eyes. They quickly surrounded the towering figure and strutted toward the gate which swung open as they approached. They didn't have to break stride. Gestapo, who else? There was no question who the visiting dignitary was. Max Schmeling, the famous boxer! Well, I'll be damned! Max Schmeling had come to visit Stalag Luft One. Why? Whose morale was being boosted? Certainly not that of the Americans. What followed disgusted me. Some American POW's came rushing up to him.

"Max, how are you? Good to see you. How about an autograph, Max?"

Max Schmeling, Hitler's symbol of German superiority until he was deposed by the great Joe Lewis, was being fawned upon by American kids in Germany. In a German prison camp. Max Schmeling and the Gestapo. Talk about false idols.

THE JEWISH BARRACKS AND
CAPT. MARGOLIN

Capt. Margolin was the ranking officer in the Jewish barracks. Margolin took charge immediately. In no uncertain terms, he outlined our situation. "Fellas, this situation stinks! I'm not going to pull punches! We are sitting on a bomb with a short fuse. We don't know what the damn Krauts have in store for us, but we ought to prepare for the worst. We will not submit to being marched off in the middle of the night. Understood?"

A voice from the group said, "Cap, what's the difference, day time, night time? Dead is dead, right?"

"If they're gonna take us down," Margolin said, "I want the rest of the camp to know about it. I don't like the idea of just disappearing from the face of the earth. I want others to know that we were once here. Just call me sentimental.

"And furthermore, if they try to move us en masse, in the middle of the night, we go down fighting, understood? If they're gonna take us down, some of them are gonna die too. We'll give them a fight, *fa schtast*? Understood?"

Capt. Margolin was one tough Jew. His hide had been toughened on the mean streets of New York City. He was an educated man whose years of learning were hidden by a gruff exterior. Passages from Shakespeare were his way of making a point. One of his favorites was from the *The Tempest*, often directed at those who fell short of his expectations: "Misery acquaints a man with strange bedfellows." It was a quotation that had comic proportions, coming at you in a strong New York accent.

NOT A BOYS' SUMMER CAMP

By and large the boys that flew our planes and fought our wars were young, unsophisticated warriors who learned the mechanics of war and used them with a skill that radiates from a young body. That is the beauty of youth. The young are graceful, fearless, indestructible fighting machines. Add a few years to their lives and they become cautious, calculating and not so eager to jump into the breach. They are now ready to point the way for other young men to take their places. To line them up and let some die.

War, and particularly combat, culminating in incarceration, drove people to do things that they ordinarily would have never dreamt of doing. I know now that which I considered battle fatigue was in reality depression.

It was rampant. It took on many faces. The bravado of the American kids was merely a cover for deeply held feelings of fear. Fear of never going home, never seeing family again. This fear was worse than death to many. Going home was the ultimate goal. Everything paled by comparison.

I often felt that a closely related matter to going home was the fear of being forgotten... left forever in this God-forsaken land... that I had never existed... that there was no home to go to... that I was invisible. Time spent as a POW gave rise to an awful feeling of being invisible and thus ignored. This is akin to being forgotten.

Look at us now; we are old men, those of us who are still left, but we made it. We are home. We are home. Sometimes I still can't believe it.

DECADES LATER

*On March 17, 2007, Leo, then 87, was awarded the Purple
Heart, European/African/Middle East Theatre Medal with 1
Bronze Star, Asiatic Pacific Theater Medal with 2 Bronze Stars,
and Prisoner of War Medal in a special ceremony at Travis Air
Force Base, Fairfield, California. The following is his address
on that occasion:*

"I'm humbled by... by this ceremony... by this entire affair.
Never in my wildest imagination could I have dreamed of
such a heart-stirring ceremony. The Air Force does indeed
take care of its own, and I'm proud to be counted among
the men and women of the United States Air Force — to be
treated as one of their own. I'm grateful that Congresswoman
Tauscher got behind me, as one of her constituents, and
used her good offices to carry out the necessary requirements
imposed by military regulations. Things that I was unable to
do by myself.

"I'm only sorry that this played out as if the military was
somehow delinquent in its duty to pin a Purple Heart on
my chest 62 years ago. Nothing could be farther from the
truth. The fault lies with the German Luftwaffe, and with me,
personally. The Germans didn't leave a medical paper trail so
I couldn't comply with the needs of the U.S. Army.

"When I was shot down, I was in the United States Army
Air Corps and I wore a khaki uniform which has since turned
into a blue uniform. Then I was dumped into Stalag Luft One,
a POW camp under the control of the German Luftwaffe and
joined 10,000 other American and British flying officers. I
was unaware of any medical facilities in this POW camp.

Bum legs and a screwed up back didn't seem like a big deal at the time. There were other things more threatening to my well-being.

"During an interrogation at Frankfurt-au-Main, the Luftwaffe's main interrogation center, the Germans made threatening references to my Jewish heritage. After that I was constantly on guard. When the Germans took the two hundred of us and put us in a separate building, (the so-called Jewish barracks) I had more on my mind than seeking out medical attention or finding out if there were indeed any medical facilities. I never did know for sure. I simply didn't want any more contact with the Germans than was absolutely necessary. An out of sight out of mind kind of thing.

"As it turned out the Soviet Army got to us before the Germans could carry out their nefarious plans. They, the Soviets, liberated us on May 1st, 1945. The story goes that the segregation of the 200 Jews was for the convenience of the Germans. When the Germans got around to it, we would be gathered up into a nice tight little group to be marched off to... oblivion.

"Long story short, here I am, at Travis Air Force Base, surrounded by friends and family. The Air Force is also my family. I'm home now; I'm home... and damned glad to be here. Thank you for this magnificent memory, thank you for the honor you have bestowed upon me. Thank you for including me in the United States Air Force family."

NOTE: *Leo and fellow POWs were liberated by the Soviet Red Army in May of 1945. Soon, with a wife and two children and a penchant for getting involved, Leo headed west and continued to make his presence known — i.e. as a Berkeley politician in the '60's, as a long time columnist, as the admired 'grandfather' of the Writers Group and author of* Going Home, *his WWII autobiography. Of the war, he says "The horrors of it have an ugly habit of dribbling down on you, drop by drop. A little here, a little there. Some would say oozing is a more descriptive word. In any event, it makes you feel dirty; it has a lasting effect and takes a lifetime getting clean."*

1943, Rapid City, South Dakota

Leo's Army Air Corps Crew, assembled for the first time and assigned their plane. Leo is in the first row middle; Bernie Blanche is in the back row, far left.

German I.D. document taken from the camp files after the POW's were liberated by the Russians and the Germans had fled.

Photo and documents provided by the author

Translated German Document

**REPORT OF CAPTURE OF MEMBERS OF
ENEMY AIR FORCES**

POST: Airbase headquarters A (e) 23/111
PLACE: V E L E O V W/L
DATE: CRASH: downed it can be taken for
granted, that the prisoner is a member of the
B-17F No. B714-E B.D.V. -75 05-501 shot down
on 11, April 44 at about 12:00 near the
forester's house ALTENICH south of WEISS-
VASSER

REGARDING CH LANDING

NAME: (last surname) BACH
FIRST: LEO S. Lt.
SERIAL NUMBER: 0-753122 T 42 - 43 O
RESULT: Captured
PLACE AND TIME OF CAPTURE: ca. 13 April 44
in the forest between WEISSELN and GEISNIG
by Mrs. ALMA SCHNAKEH. Delivered to
Prisoner of War Camp.

NAME OF HOSPITAL
PLACE, DATE AND TIME OF INTERNMENT

German document chronicling Leo's capture.

EILEEN SCHNEPP looks too young to have been involved in any WWII stories. She has an effervescent personality and an expressive way of reacting to the stories read in class. Little David is her remembrance of what the war did to her as a very young girl dealing with the war from the safety of the United States. But the ocean could not separate the pain that her parents suffered watching events unfold from that safety.

LITTLE DAVID

The staccato radio voice had become a house sound like the opening and closing of drawers, the water running in the sink, and the jangling of cutlery and dishes. I remember that particular early summer morning even though it was long ago, 1940. As I sit here, I can still breathe the pungent smell of onions as well as the fragrance of hot chocolate.

My bedroom was next to the kitchen. I woke up to these sounds and smells. Often I would scrunch down under the blankets to avoid both the icy linoleum and my parents. But today was sunny, and I had plans to go swimming at the park pool. Boston had a hot, humid climate in the summer. My skinny ten-year-old body flew into the kitchen with my nightgown billowing around me.

I looked carefully at my father seated at the table and then at my mother who had turned away from the stove to stare at me. Her look told me that the war was going badly, and my father was a tinder box. I never deliberately tried to provoke him, but my very presence seemed to unearth conflicts that I didn't understand.

Quietly I sat down opposite the hunched figure that was my father. I looked into the plate of hot oatmeal that my mother had put in front of me. Droplets of sweat were starting to run down the back of my neck. It was summer. It was hot. My irritation overcame my good sense.

I was not going to say a word, but I did, "Why can't I have cold cereal?" He lifted his head and glared at me. I shrank into my seat readying myself for the battery of words. He had an actor's booming voice and dramatic facial expressions and gestures. I was about to become his audience. He stood up and hovered over me.

"The Queen of Sheba doesn't want the cereal her mother made for her. Do you think your mother was cooling herself at the stove? No, she was making sure that you had food in your stomach. There are thousands of children, even your cousins, who do not have any cereal, any food for their empty stomachs. Do you know that there is a war going on?" He raised my head, pulling my hair, as he said the last sentence.

I stammered, "Yes, I'm sorry," and lowered my face to the dish of steaming cereal. I kept my head down until I heard his heavy footsteps and the bang of a closing door. My mother sat down next to me. She lifted my chin and said, "Yittele, darling, you must not think that he does not love you. He does. He came here to be with you and left his mother and four sisters. To be here with you he gave up his acting to be a common house painter. We must make up for what he has lost. Be patient."

When I came home for lunch after swimming in the park, I saw my mother reading a letter with her lips pursed and her eyes squinting. Then she folded the letter on her lap and nodded her head exclaiming, "I do not believe it. It is impossible." A picture was lying on the floor. I picked it up and saw Little David for the first time.

I put the picture of a round-faced, chubby child in front of her face and asked, "Who is this?" She seemed dazed, and I shook her arm.

"Oh," she said, "this is your cousin."

I was screaming. "Who are his parents? Where are they? Are they in the war?"

My mother laughed. "Let me catch my breath. Your father will be home soon. I cannot wait to tell him the good news. Yes, they are in the war, but they are alive. We were sure that they were dead, but no, they escaped from Poland and the Nazis and fled into Russia. This little baby," the picture shook in her hand as she grabbed it from me, "is the son of your father's sister, Hava, and her husband."

I was jumping and twirling in circles. Something good had happened in our family. Maybe now we could be happy. Mother was laughing. Things were changing.

I stopped my gyrations to ask, "When are they coming here?"

Putting her hand over her mouth, my mother erased the laugh and replaced it with the same flat lines that her lips had formed over the last year. Things had not changed, but maybe they would when the baby came to America.

I put an arm around my mother's shoulder and murmured

into her ear, "He can sleep in my room. I will take care of him."

She kissed the hand that hung over her shoulder and replied, "You are a good girl, but do not think too much about your cousin. There are many difficulties. Now, have something to eat."

The wall between my bedroom and the kitchen was so thin that I could hear every word they spoke as they stirred the pale tea in tall glasses with a sugar cube in the bottom. My father's voice invaded my room, and my mother's soft murmurings were a reassuring counterpoint. Sometimes I would fall asleep as my mother spoke, only to be awakened by my father's thundering voice.

"Why did she leave my mother? Why did she get married? And a baby! So much foolishness! Hava was smart. I do not understand. She promised to take care of my mother before I left."

"Darling, she writes about this in her letter." I could hear the rustling of paper and then my mother reading, "Mama died in her sleep. As you know, she was very sick. Thank God the Nazis did not get her. I was able to run away with Ben right after the funeral before the Germans came into Nashelsk. As you know, we have been both sweethearts and communists for many years. We saw this as an opportunity to go to Russia, a dream we both had. After a long march with our comrades through the woods of Poland, we are finally in paradise. Ben and I were married right away, and we were soon blessed with a healthy baby boy. Our comrades are taking care of us, and we are fine. Please do not worry about us."

"Those Russian comrades will kill them. Do they really believe that the Russians have stopped hating the Jews? They are fools, and I cannot do anything." The sentence ended with a moan.

"Darling, I heard Joe Korn talking about taking his niece from Russia to Japan and then into Canada. We will see him on Sunday. You can ask him. It is too soon to give up hope. Hope is all we have."

"When I left Poland, just two years ago, I knew what Hitler would do to the Jews. Yet I left my family, oh Hava, and came to America to live with strangers."

"Shh, the child will hear you. Now, let us go to bed."

My mother's reassurances calmed my fears. I told myself that I would never lose hope about Little David. Before I went to sleep I mentally rearranged my room so that there would be space for a crib. Then as I closed my eyes, I heard my father's words again. True, I hadn't seen him until I was seven. It was just my mother and me. But was I a stranger?

The next Sunday I tried to hear the conversation between my father and Mr. Korn, but I didn't understand all of it. However, my parents embraced each other and laughed afterwards, so I decided that I had better get ready for Little David. For the next few weeks the volume on the radio was lower, and my parents spirits were higher.

My own plans were frequently disrupted. On my way out the door for my weekly visit to the library, I felt my mother's hand on my arm and heard her say, "Get your beach things, we are going to Uncle Sam's."

"Great!" I responded, and I returned to my room to gather my beach bag and throw my books on the bed. I loved Revere Beach which not only had a white sand approach to gentle waves but an amusement park, too. My uncle always gave me a half-dollar, enough for a hot dog with soda and maybe a ball for Little David. In my ten-year-old mind things happened quickly. My cousin could crawl into my room one day next week.

Finding a ball for a baby was not as easy as I had thought. It couldn't be so small that he could choke on it or too big for him to grasp. In a souvenir shop I saw a brightly colored ball that was just the right size. For now, he would be able to turn it over and gurgle with delight at the colors, and later, when he could walk, we would roll it between our outstretched legs. I could see us playing catch on the front lawn. He had sturdy little legs, and he giggled every time he caught the ball.

After the trip to Revere Beach, my mother took me to see the great uncles, the rich ones. They gave me money, too. I hoped that they also gave some to my mother. From the talk I had overheard at home, I knew that the plan to get Little David and his parents out of Russia cost a lot of money.

These uncles had two grandsons that were my age. I had hoped to see them, but they took off on their bicycles as soon as they saw me. I would never have a bicycle. They cost too much, and they were dangerous, particularly for a girl. But Little David would ride a bike — a Speedo.

Almost a year went by. My parents were waiting anxiously for another letter from Hava, but it never came. Meanwhile, Little David was growing older. I would have to get a stroller for him so we could go on walks together. We would go to Franklin Park. I would let him out of the stroller to run around in the place with the arched bridge and the stream that ran over colored rocks. Of course, he would walk towards the water, but I would grab him and swing him.

The war was even more troubling, and it looked as though Germany was winning the war. I had to find a way to get Little

David to America. My magic hadn't worked. I had wished on the first star, crossed all my fingers, hadn't stepped on cracks in the sidewalk, and called on God's help. Even my atheist parents talked a lot about God. Maybe he would spare one small child, even though millions were dying.

The feel-good movies of the decade gave me an idea. Wishing real hard could make things come true. Instead of clapping my feet together like Dorothy, I would squeeze my eyes tightly and imagine my little cousin, my brother, my child. I would try to feel his firm little body as I hugged him. I would listen for the sound of his giggle. I could almost feel his curly hair slip through my fingers. I did this several times a day and just before going to sleep.

Then one morning in June I was blasted out of sleep by the screaming radio. The words, "Germany has marched into Russia," were repeated again and again. This was bad news. I slowly opened the door to the kitchen, afraid to look at the faces of my parents.

Tears were running down my father's cheeks, and he was sobbing. "Hava is dead. Soon we will all be dead."

My mother had her arms around his shoulders, and she was murmuring, "Shh, shh, shh, do not give up hope so quickly. Russia is a big country with a big army. They can fight back. Remember what happened to Napoleon. May the Germans freeze into stones in Russia."

I could see that it was hard for my father to leave the house to go to work. He stood in the middle of the kitchen with a dazed expression and with his lunch pail dangling from a lifeless hand. I touched the back of his belt and said, "Daddy, I can give you an English lesson tonight."

He turned towards me. He looked puzzled, and then he

sighed and patted my head. "Yes, before I die, I should learn English from my American daughter." And then he bent down, kissed me on my forehead and said, "You are a good girl." Swiftly, he left the house. On that awful day I became my father's daughter.

Finally, the war did end. I was fifteen and thinking of big boys. But Little David came quickly back into my thoughts when my parents hired an organization that searched for refugees. There was no trace of our families. They had just disappeared. I couldn't accept that. My Little David was somewhere. He was not dead.

Even now, when David would be in his sixties, I question anyone I meet who was in the Holocaust. I ask them where they lived and the name of their mother. I am still searching for Little David.

NOTE: When Eileen moved to Rossmoor in 2007, the first thing she did, even before unpacking, was to find a writers' group. Convinced it would be a community of bright, interesting people, she wasn't disappointed. Eileen's writing reflects her belief that her early experiences gave her empathy and the desire to make the world a better place. She has worked as a Special Education teacher, specializing in learning disabilities, and as a consultant and writer for textbook publishers. She describes herself as a survivor and an illegal immigrant, having arrived from Poland in utero, unbeknownst to Ellis Island officials.

ADRIENNE WOLFERT is so petite she is nearly swallowed up by the dais as she reads softly into the mike. She nearly always needs to be reminded to speak up a bit louder, but each of her stories has you leaning in to be sure you do not miss a word. This story of what was going on here in the U.S. of A. during WWII is surely no exception.

REMINGTON ARMS: THE WAR EFFORT

Imagine medieval turrets, towers, and stone arches. The greatest arms plant in the United States was called Aladdin's Castle! It covered forty acres of land and had a million and a half feet of floor space. It supplied America and her allies through two world wars, among other feats. The quick resurgence of our country's industry spurred the victory over the Nazis. The Remington Arms Company of Bridgeport, Connecticut was the largest contributor!

It was summer, 1942. I was eighteen and wanted to go to college but couldn't afford the $25 tuition at our state school. At 60 cents an hour, 80 cents for night work, I saw great possibilities. I hopped on a bus from my 40 cents an hour department store wage, already an hour's ride from my home in Trumbull. It would take over two hours traveling time each way to Remington. Eventually, it was closer to three hours, not too pleasant on the 11-7 graveyard shift.

But I didn't care anything about that as I joined the excited crowds of job seekers waiting four deep for two blocks. The country was still suffering from the effects of the Great Depression, and the tension was building. I was surprised to be picked from the line six hours later.

After passing an extensive mental and physical exam, as tough as anything I'd experienced before, I was assigned to the 7-3 shift the next day.

Remington had 17,000 employees. At the gate the next morning, thousands of people poured out of the 11-7 shift as thousands were struggling to get in. I was lost in the surge of workers. Everyone seemed bigger and older than I. Somehow I found myself in a smaller group.

"Follow me," a uniformed man barked. I couldn't take my eyes off the gun on his hip. "Keep your eyes straight ahead. Don't look right or left!"

We marched behind him. The noise of the factory hit me like a physical force. Once I sneaked a look and saw that we were passing a stadium sized department filled with gigantic and grotesque machines. The operators had to climb ladders to reach their seats. They looked like tiny figures. But those tiny figures manipulated those behemoths that pressed gun powder into the tiny shell casings I would be inspecting. Soon, my sister would join those workers.

A woman marching behind me pressed my shoulder. I couldn't hear the guard, but she shouted in my ear that I was receiving a sharp reprimand for "gawking."

I was led to a large room lined with benches... my department I was told. I am an inspector. A bin of glittering objects that turned out to be tracer bullet casings was placed in front of each bench. I don't know how many benches there were in that area. Figuring that the plant was forty acres with a million and a half feet of work space, there were probably thousands of bench workers.

We were not allowed to leave our benches even for lunch. Bring a sandwich. The bell rang for "rest periods." If we needed to go to the ladies' room any other time, we had to request a guard. He wore guns, too. This proved embarrassing for me, and puzzling, because the bathrooms had both toilets and urinals. Did men and women share the bathrooms? I thought the guard had made a mistake. However, I made no comment.

Our job was to inspect tracer bullets for flaws. You picked up a handful, rolled them from one hand to the other until they appeared joined into one piece, a golden bracelet. Watch for spots or dents. Throw away any duds. Every half-hour, the inspector came to review the work at random. If he found a dud in your bin, back went the whole thousand for review.

I was very ambitious the first day and filled more boxes than the other inspectors.

At lunch time, I slowly became aware that two women were standing, one on either side of me, glaring, as I bit into my peanut butter sandwich.

"The quota is 26,500 a day," one said. "If you do more, they'll raise it. We don't get paid for extra, young lady."

"You are probably working to go to college," said the other. "We are working to support our families while our men are away."

That was my first brush with a strong labor union. I slowed down — quickly.

Expertly spilling the bullets from one hand to the other, concentrating on looking for imperfections, I was Rosie the Riveter.

After a few days, my eyes burned, my back hurt. Two buses and a half mile walk to get home. It was at least a twelve hour stretch, sometimes more. The changing shifts did me in. When I seemed to adjust to the hours, I was changed to another shift. I either got up or came home at dawn. I could not sleep during the daylight. But the idea of quitting never occurred to me.

I never thought I would feel nostalgia for Aladdin's Castle, but when I heard it was abandoned and burned in a fire last year, I mourned. I think because working in it made me part of the "war effort." Boys could be soldiers, and this was what girls could do to help.

This was the mood of the time. Neighbors became friends and strangers became neighbors. Foreign countries became "us," their defeats and victories, "ours." The Gold Star in the window was the boy we all remembered. The war effort joined us.

Today, our world is still at war. I feel that desire again, but curiously estranged. I am beyond helping this "war effort" of the 21st century. Not that anyone has asked me for my help. Except for separating bottles and cans from newspapers and garbage, I'm doing little. We are not even asked to save gas or in any way to curb our extravagant excesses.

But in those days, in that war, we were all in it. Every child, every teenager, every grandma and grandpa, looked to do his or her part in the "war effort." Maybe it didn't mean much, just covering the windows at night, or collecting metal trash, or cutting coupons for rationed food and gas, but it was an involvement we all wanted with our soldiers. And it added up.

We won.

NOTE: Adrienne, a native of Connecticut, received a BA from Barnard College and a MFA from Vermont College. She has authored three novels and several books of poetry. At the invitation of William Meredith, poet laureate of America, her poems have been recorded at the Library of Congress. Sponsored by the Virginia Center for the Creative Arts she had a particularly exciting fellowship to Peredelkino, Russia, a writer's retreat near Boris Pasternack's home outside Moscow. She was there, "a guest of the ghosts of Chekhov and Tolstoi," as she describes it, when President Reagan visited the Soviet Union and Leonid Breshnev resigned. Currently she is short story editor for At Home and Abroad.

Remington Pledge to Victory Campaign Goes Over the Top

The Pledge To Victory campaign of the Remington Arms Co. went over the top with a bang. The above photo shows part of the tour of the plant on Pledge To Victory Day

"Miss Remington Patriot" who with "Uncle Sam" was one of the features of the victory parade

Newspaper clipping of the day

HELMUT UNBEHOVEN was inducted into the German Luftwaffe as a so-called "Luftwaffen Helper" in 1942. He was 15 years old. His sister, Irmhild Epstein, author of Wolf Whistles and Looting, *asked him to write of his experiences during that horrible time. The following is her translation of what he wrote.*

LOOKING BACK IS NOT RECOMMENDED

1942 - 1944

I spoke with two young guys today, over coffee. The conversation turned to the time of my youth. I told them I had no youth, and I explained why.

"What was it like," they asked with utter incredulity, "when you were only 15, and you were trained to man a flak canon and shoot at enemy bombers night after night? Weren't you still in school? Didn't your parents protest?"

Well, yes, we were, and yes, they did. Let me try to tell you what it was like. Yes, my father and others got together and wrote long, polite (you had to be polite, meaning careful, when addressing Nazi authority) letters describing the hardships their children suffered, and wouldn't they serve the Fatherland better, alive and in school, etc.

A stronger protest and plea also went to the director of the school, a private high school, or gymnasium, as it was called, asking him for help, but all in vain.

Those letters, by the way, are still in my father's carefully collected records. So are my own, written in a matter-of-fact style, in pencil, showing still childish, 15-year-old handwriting, without complaints, whining or sentimentality, just to inform, and stay in touch with my father. My father, who was such a rock and reliable anchor, the father without whom I might not have survived.

So, our personal lives were simply taken from us. They just didn't exist anymore. We marched everywhere together: to eat, to the weekly shower, everywhere. From the age of fifteen to seventeen we didn't take one step in privacy. In the morning we marched to our school classes in the dining room of a nearby inn. Our teachers had to travel an hour from Altenburg, my home town, to Leipzig and walk out to our barracks.

Our helmets and gas masks lay on the tables next to our school books, always at the ready, as we might be called to "fire-readiness" at any moment. During the night, we were sometimes called two or even three times. We were always sleepy.

As soon as the English or American bomber units — the English at night, the Americans punctually at midday — flew over German territory, we were the first to be informed and ordered to our flaks. Then, and only then, did the truly hellish howls of hundreds of sirens from Leipzig and surrounding towns start.

"Alarm ready" meant we had to run, often half asleep, to the canons, while "fire ready" meant the munitions were to be locked into the breach. Then, almost at once, we would hear the steady, endless humming from 800 or 900 or more B17 Flying Fortresses, Lancasters, Liberators, Short Sterlings, etc. Each one carried 4,000 kilograms of explosives. Sometimes, for special attacks, for instance Dresden, they followed up with 300,000 to 400,000 fire bombs. That way the water mains were destroyed first, and fighting the fires became impossible. With this carefully planned method, 35,000 souls perished in Dresden on that one horrific night.

Every 8.8 centimeter canon was manned with five 15-year-olds. Only the "Kl," who actually put the shell into the gun, was a "real soldier." That was because when the gun pointed straight up, it was too heavy for us to lift the shells. After a prolonged firing the guns glowed a bright pinkish/red inside the barrels. During the longest action every gun shot 300 rounds of 8.8 shells into the air. Their splinters came down again with a noisy, high pitched chirping sound. The shell casings piled up so high that we kept stumbling over them.

Of course, we never stopped or prevented any bomb attacks like those on Halle, Leipzig, Leuna, or the Junkers factories, etc. What arrogance and insanity to assume that we could!

Six 8.8 flak canons were dug into a wheat field, and 4 other units were measuring distance, heights and other values. I was part of the measuring unit. Next to this we had built up a little hill, upon which our commander could stand, looking into the sky through his binoculars, and direct our fire when the enemy came into our sights. Six little white puffs of smoke appeared above, below and between the B17 Fortress formations. These puffs measured the altitude, airspeed and heading of the fortresses. Again and again we fired. But they just kept calmly flying on.

I sometimes sat at the radio to report sightings of new squadrons and other information by code names. For instance "rain on the roof" meant bombs falling on Leipzig. This info I had to call up to the lieutenant on the hill, who then ordered new firing directions. Or sometimes the order would be "stop firing," if the enemy came in a direct flight toward us. Then we had to take cover.

When we attended our lessons, half asleep in our makeshift classrooms, and the siren blasted, we pushed aside our school books, grabbed helmets and gas masks, and dashed to our flak positions, past the teacher, who sat there sadly looking after his boys, and yet was unable to do anything about the insanity all around him. The teachers, by the way, were also given helmets, and assigned a special ditch for cover when the bomb attacks came.

And they came. The whole sky would be full of little planes, like toys, hundreds of them, orderly, in triangle formation. The blue sky was combed through with countless white lines of contrails. Protective fighter planes, Mustangs or Lightnings, were covering their flanks. German fighter planes were seldom seen after 1943. The roaring became louder and louder. Our first volley started booming into the sky. Our teacher took cover in his ditch. This was the normal daily course of events in our lives.

One day we were transferred onto the roof of a manufacturing plant of the Junkers Airplane Works near Leipzig. We placed boards (the same as those with which we had built our tiny barracks) over the glass roof leading to the canons, so we wouldn't fall through.

These were lighter guns, with four barrels, 2 centimeters

each, and we could load them ourselves. My friend, Klaus Amdt, was the "Kl" in charge. He showed no fear — firing away as if it were a game. He was my age. I admired his courage.

Then came the day of the great direct attack by the American B17 bombers. It was February 20, 1944. Luckily, we had been moved back onto the ground. It was a beautiful, sunny day, blue sky, midday. Hundreds of Fortresses flew above us. The corporal, who was watching through the flak telescope, said, "They are opening the bomb flaps."

We looked up. Suddenly I saw something glitter, like a bunch of needles thrown into the air. I heard the lieutenant scream: "Full cover!"

Then the bursts and crashes thundered all around us, an indescribable racket, like a fast train approaching while you're lying on the tracks— and then, nothing. Everything went still and dark.

The next thing I saw, as I came to, was a crater six meters deep right next to me. A gun barrel lay at its bottom. Alex and Dimitri, our two Russian prisoners, dug me out.

A 500 kilogram bomb had hit our gun position, producing a kind of earth hill all around, under which I had been buried. I saw Klaus walking around dazed, and Schmidt trying to remove his helmet. It was dented in and stuck to his head.

The earth, a few minutes ago still white from the February snow, was now black. Smoke from fires everywhere darkened the sun. Out of earth holes and bomb craters all around me, crawled confused, dirt covered figures, my class mates! No one was dead! The pain in my back immobilized me. But when we all found each other — it is true — we laughed.

We counted 24 bomb craters between our 3 gun positions,

which stood 30 meters apart in a triangular formation.

But all around us were the dead, without arms, without heads. The Junker factory was gone. A gigantic, spiraling cloud of black smoke was the only indication of where it had once stood. Late explosions still crackled and popped.

A corporal from Pomerania, stubbornly, kept digging in the earth, field telephone in one hand, searching for the torn wire with the other. He found it and connected it, turned the crank, and said in a matter-of-fact tone of voice, "Fourth company destroyed," and hung up.

That really said it all. Destroyed. Everything. Our barracks, built by ourselves when we got there, to be near our canons, were now heaps of boards and splinters.

One B17 bomber came flying very low and slow towards us. What did he want? To finish us off? Or maybe to photograph the scene to show "mission accomplished?"

Klaus ran to a still standing gun, trying to shoot. It was jammed and didn't work. The Fortress banked slowly over the inferno and then disappeared.

One of our guys lost it and ran around screaming. Another came staggering towards us. He had been thrown 10 meters into the air. I don't remember who it was.

Another barracks, a little sturdier than ours, was some distance from us. It housed the female air force helpers, girls our age, who worked the measuring instruments.

There had been a Christmas party a couple of months back, and we were all invited. The tables were decorated with white napkins and green fir twigs. I was seated next to Renate von Leibnitz, and she had looked at me with that special smile. What did I know about life? Nothing…!

The girls' barracks were burnt to the ground, black smoke

belching from the ruins. I shoved a long board under my arm as a crutch, and hobbled through the eerie, blackened moonscape, screaming for Renate. But I never found her again.

Then a jeep pulled up, a major got out and handed us tablets of fructose. Fructose? For energy, I guess. It was something. We dug around in what once were our barracks, loaded anything personal on a little hand cart and moved on.

I dropped my water bottle. It fell onto a corpse without a head. I picked it up again, took a sip, and dragged myself on with the others.

My thoughts were of Renate. A girl— it was something so foreign to me... so pure, so sweet... so beautiful! She had poured thin cocoa for me from a pewter pot... .

Actually, I wasn't supposed to be at that Christmas party, because I had criticized a Hitler song during a music lesson. It was only the grammar I corrected, but that was sufficient to cause that low ranking Nazi leader (not one of our gymnasium teachers) to punish me with guard duty on Christmas. But someone with a higher rank must have overruled him, since I was allowed to go after all.

By luck I sat next to Renate. My heart jumped and wouldn't be still! She really sat there next to me. It was not a dream, her light hair, her smell, her soft voice. So that's what it was, life. That's what we didn't know.

She led me into the barracks' kitchen and poured me a cup of cocoa. She looked at me with her smiling eyes. That was all.

And now I searched for her. In vain.

We were sent back to new flak positions. Klaus and I were

still together. I was still hobbling on my crutch. We kept firing. We starved. We were always tired, so tired – so tired of everything. If only we could sleep, that's all we thought about.

We had no idea that a nation, ours, had collapsed, that we would all be criminals soon.

That the world would be partitioned anew, that Deutschland, "*heilig Vaterland*" (as we still had sung) was no more.

Five years later, nobody would care to hear about or remember the catastrophe that had brought us all to the abyss. Just five short years later, everybody would start again. Exactly as before. Wishing and working only for the so called "good life."

In short: repress, forget — everything — and as quickly as possible!

Life must go on, mustn't it?

Nobody cared about us. Our youth, which we gave so obediently. Marching, firing, enduring and experiencing untold hardships and misery. Not realizing, we were already in the beyond, where other generations of our age, were just starting to come of age. We were already past death, when the so-called peaceful life, this unspeakably stupid, material, mindless, middle-class business of "making money" started again. The *Wirtschaftswunder* (economic miracle) was in full progress.

Surely, we too, adapted… as was expected. We did as we were told. We felt as we were told to feel, hated and shunned. We lost the war. Worse, *we* killed six million Jews. *WE* were now the pariahs of the earth!

So pretend nothing had happened, not the destruction,

the theft of our youth, the youth of a whole generation!

And now appeared the new "cool" generation. We let them have the field. No problem. What did they know? But what can one do without the ability to deny oneself... ? I can't. Not much longer. The end is in sight.

"How much I would like to drink a few glasses of wine with you once more, Klaus... ."

But Klaus is somewhere up north managing a gas station. He serves the chic generation with their Audis and Porsches. One jokes, one laughs. Why? We're still alive! Hurrah!

What? Life? Where is our life?

It was taken from us.

Can we ever forget the horror that was committed in our name? We were cruelly deceived, but deceived no one.

We were unsuspecting and believed in music, poetry, and dreamed of girls and romance. Can we ever believe again? Can anybody believe in us again?

We didn't even complain, not once, not ever about our cheated life. What good would it have done? Who cared to hear it? We accepted, from childhood on, everything. We trusted and believed.

But now, one of us should stand up and blow everything to kingdom-come! All of the hypocrisy, pretensions, masquerades and lies!

But they would just continue to come back... like one of those little men that get up again no matter how often you knock them down.

So everything stays the same, only with a different name. So what's the point?

Let's have another glass of wine!

NOTE: Helmut returned home on foot and alone at war's end and soon graduated valedictorian of his class. After four friends were convicted of dispensing "freedom" leaflets and executed by order of a Russian tribunal, he escaped to the West and became a journalist for Die Welt *in Hamburg. He finally settled in a Black Forest village where he pursued his loves: writing, reading, especially philosophers, and art. Death was the main theme of his particularly striking etchings. Despite his eccentricities, the villagers fed and helped him. He died and was buried in their churchyard at age 61. His sister, Irmhild Epstein, is still welcomed there.*

The following letters are among the many written on Helmut's behalf during his time as a so-called Luftwaffen Helper and preserved by his family these last sixty-six years. They have been translated by his sister. The phrase "Heil Hitler" found at the closing of each letter was the requirement at the time.

Altenburg, Dec. 27, 1943
Dear Dr. Fritzsche,

In response to your questions about the well-being and whereabouts of our children, I'd like to answer you at length.

The boys survived the terror attack on Leipzig rather well. In general they are doing fine, but much is left to be desired.

Your personal interest did the boys a lot of good, emotionally. But even at that time the necessary care of food and equipment was very, very sparse.

One should remember that these boys are students, children even! If you could take a look around their barracks, see what their clothes look like, what the boys are wearing on their bodies, (their socks are such as they might have been wearing years ago) you would understand with what mixed feelings the parents view the so-called care their boys receive. The parents are doing what they can even in these hard times, but what these children are getting is not what was promised them. It wouldn't be so bad if at least their schooling weren't so pathetic. They cannot do their homework as there is not enough room at a proper table, nor is there enough daylight. Is it any wonder that those who might have considered a career as officers, have changed their minds?

The present situation can simply not continue like this. These are children who are in urgent need of schooling. What shall become of them if they become drafted or members of the RAD (*Reichsarbeitsdienst, a sort of working troupe, before the actual military*) without a proper High School finish? The children are worse off than elementary students, who after they finish at 14, still can enter a trade school.

Our sons' education, through the failure of the Ernestinum, is so totally neglected that they will find it difficult later in life to succeed in their choice of profession.

It is wrong to treat these young students like ordinary Infantry recruits. They are only 16-years-old and, although nobody wants to complain, least of all the kids, my concern for their future lets me pour out my heart to you, dear Oberstudienrat, in the hope that you can still use your influence to guide their lives in more appropriate directions.

Heil Hitler!
Fritz Klingsporn, Regierungsoberinspector (*and father of a high school classmate of Helmut's*)

Altenburg, Dec. 28, 1943
Dear Dr. Fritzsche,
Director Ernestinum (*a private high school*)

After the high school asked parents about the well-being of the airforce helpers, our children, I took the liberty to explain the situation without exaggeration.

Scholastically the children are grossly neglected. Whose fault this is I cannot ascertain, but it can certainly not hurt to see to it that the responsible military faction is made aware of this. I add a copy of my letter and assume and hope that you already took the necessary action.

Hopefully the petition will have the desired effect, because things simply cannot continue like this, as the boys must become emotionally and intellectually stunted.

Heil Hitler!
Fritz Klingsporn, Regierungsoberinspector
Alvin Unbehaun* (*Helmut's father*)

*Helmut changed the spelling of his name in his mid-twenties when he began writing.

Written by Dr. Fritzsche sometime during December, 1943:

ERNESTINUM (State High School for Boys)
To: The parents of our LWH - Class 6a
   Since Nov. 12, 1943, our LWHs, Class 6a, were moved
from their military location to a new one near Leipzig. All
schooling had to stop since then. We don't even know exactly
to which locations of Leipzig our students have been moved.
In spite of several written requests we did not receive an
answer. The military station L16 197 didn't even, upon my
pleading, tell me their superior military station or give me
their telephone number. They only told me that notification
would come when scholastic instruction will become possible
again. Of course I informed the Minister for Education of
this strange situation. I also received no information about
the well-being of our students even after the bomb attack on
Leipzig. Therefore I ask you please to let me know where I
can reach your son and where in Leipzig he is stationed and
how he is doing.
   You will see from my writing that the school has done
everything it possibly could.

Heil Hitler!
Dr. Fritzsche (*Director of the school*)

JULES SCHWARTZ'S wife, PEARL, insists her only role in Journey of Intrigue *was to assemble husband Jules' sporadic notes of the last twenty years into a cohesive chronicle of army memories. His notes were in competent hands: Pearl studied creative writing in Manhattan's New School for Social Research, has been published in several periodicals and produced a book of short stories describing her life in Brooklyn, New York, where she grew up in a mixed ethnic neighborhood. As an almost charter member of the Writers Group, she's especially known for her true-to-life prose and probing, constructive critiques of others' work.*

JOURNEY OF INTRIGUE

OCTOBER, 2008

I became 91 years of age in September. It has taken over 60 years, but I am determined to write my story — my experience in World War II. Mine is different from the countless stories I have read about the war. I must say right up front I'm not sure that all that I write is fact or fiction. There are so many blanks and so much that is hard to believe, I sometimes question my memories.

WORLD WAR II

I was 25 when I was inducted in January, 1943. As the sole provider for my widowed mother, I had to wait until one of the three brothers who preceded me into the army came back from the Pacific wounded. So, I was accepted. My brothers have all died by now.

We lived in New York City, and I was inducted at Whitehall Street in Manhattan. Having been a "physical culture nut," I was in very good condition except for an untreated lazy eye which did not merit rejection.

That day I was transferred to Camp Upton on Long Island where I got my uniform and shots, and took the aptitude test. Apparently, my scores were among the highest of the thousands taking the tests. In two days I was back in New York City stationed on Governor's Island in the East River. This was the end of my standard basic training.

I was assigned to a Military Police (MP) Squad responsible for guarding the General Court Prison known as Castle William. (It's still there but vacant.) However, I had no connection with the prison other than to study the courts-martial records to learn how the army treated military criminal offences. The prison was for soldiers who had or were awaiting a General Court-martial, the highest form of trial for serious crimes: desertion, rape, murder, etc. My assignment was to sit in on trials as an observer and to study transcripts of concluded General Courts-martial for experience in military law. I do not recall ever seeing the prison cells, just the records room and the cadre for the prison.

The MP prison guards had a barracks right next to the

prison. I ate, took the Public Safety course, and practiced ju-jitsu (kill blows only) with the MPs. I learned to shoot a pistol and a carbine. Although I was a PFC, I had a pass and could, and did leave the island practically at will. I went home to visit my mother frequently.

I was with the MPs for about four months. The members of this group were sons of ranking officers and wealthy families and were permanent cadres. They had super cooks, no K.P. or other duties normal to low-rank soldiers. People said one would have to earn $50,000 a year in 1943 dollars to eat as we did —with steaks and lobster, etc. Because I had no MP prison assignment, I asked for and was allowed to take a released prisoner to Camp Stoneman, a point of embarkation in California's bay area. I wanted this assignment for the adventure of traveling west, and because I was fond of a girl I knew from Salt Lake City, one of the stops on the trip. The trip was to be by railroad because planes were far too precious for such purposes.

When I reported to the prison, I was told that, normally, two MPs took a prisoner across country, but a temporary shortage of manpower dictated that I go alone. I was given a 45 automatic, a billy club and an MP armband. The prisoner had been tried for desertion, but since he was not convicted, he was reassigned to his former company overseas.

The prisoner was the largest, most powerfully built black man I had ever seen. I was required by military law to handcuff him. The cuff barely covered his wrist while I got 8 clicks, about two inches on my wrist. The penalty for losing a prisoner was to take his punishment, so on the ferry from Governor's Island to Hoboken, I gave him this speech: "I'm going to remove your handcuffs as soon as I tell you the ground rules for our trip," I said. "I'm not your judge or your jury, and I don't want this trip to be a continuation of your punishment. However, I do not intend to let you escape. I have a gun and a club and I can always cuff you again." I then removed the cuffs and put them under my coat.

In Hoboken we boarded the first train to Chicago on the Lackawanna Railroad. The conductor saw that I was with a prisoner and in for a long ride. He suggested I cuff my prisoner to a seat, so that I could roam around. I chose not to do so and stayed awake one whole day and night to guard him.

In Chicago, we had a four-hour layover, so I tried to take him to the USO (United Services Organizations). Of course, I was not allowed to enter with my prisoner, and the USO guards suggested I turn him over to the local police who would hold him for me. Again, I chose not to imprison him. Instead, I bought him a dinner at a café and we sat and talked. My prisoner told me that because I treated him so well, he would not try to escape. Of course, I had no way of judging his sincerity.

On the next train, the Union Pacific to Omaha, Nebraska, I anticipated another sleepless night, but Lady Luck smiled on me. The car we boarded was filled with several dozen tough-looking men in Navy uniforms with the Seabee insignia. The Seabees were civilians-turned-sailors assigned to build the landing strips for ships and planes in the midst of the fiercest combat areas. Among the group, I saw a familiar face, an Irishman who was as tall as he was wide and wearing a derby. I recognized him as Mike Quill, the President of New York City Transport Workers Union who built and ran the New York City subways. Quill was leading this group who were returning from leave back to the Pacific. I went to greet him, and we talked for a few minutes. He saw that I was with a prisoner, and said his very tough bunch of men would be playing cards all day and night, and that I could leave my prisoner in the middle of the car. He said I did not have to cuff him, and Quill guaranteed he'd be available all the way to North Platte, Nebraska. For the next couple of days, I was free to enjoy the trip and mix with the regular passengers. The last train we took was the Southern Pacific, and Mike Quill's attention supported me all the way.

On my trip back after delivering the prisoner to Camp Stoneman, I stopped in Salt Lake City where I saw my former girlfriend who now had two kids.

During the four months I was with the MPs, periodically, I would be called into the barracks' Day Room where I was briefed regarding the war situation by people from O.S.S., Scotland Yard, the Free French, etc. I guess I was being prepared for my predestined assignment and a totally new life with the Counter Intelligence Corps.

₧

I have long been confounded by the many instances of lost memory in regard to my wartime experience. The first of many future blanks in my memory occurred when I left the MPs to get on a Liberty Ship on the way to Europe and the war. I have no memory of how I got to the ship or whom I answered to. I do remember my ship was part of what I was told was the largest convoy to cross the Atlantic. The convoy was led by the battleship *Texas* which later led the invasion attack. I remember parts of the trip clearly, and other parts not at all.

The North Atlantic was so rough it blasted a twelve-foot

hole in the bow. I spent much time on deck watching the destroyers zooming in and out around the convoy looking for U-Boats (German submarines). I can still hear the strange sounds the destroyers made. We came down the Irish Sea. I have never seen such green water before or since. We docked in Cardiff, Wales and immediately boarded a train for Manchester, England.

In Manchester I was billeted in the home of Mrs. Barlow, the wife of the Police Chief of Manchester, along with two other army men whom I had not met before. Mrs. Barlow's two sons were stationed in India, and her husband was stationed elsewhere, involved with the war. Her teenage daughter, Gwendolyn, lived with her. Mrs. Barlow was a blustery, kindly woman who treated me and the other two servicemen as she would have treated her own sons.

I remember the first Sunday in her home. She was cooking "fried bread" (French toast) when I wandered into the kitchen.

"Jules," she said. "Would you go upstairs and knock up Gwendolyn. We're all going to church."

"But, Mrs. Barlow," I said. "I won't be joining you. I'm Jewish."

She extended her plump elbows outward and locked her fists into her sides. "And what is that supposed to mean?" she said through tight lips.

Needless to say, after breakfast, I and the two other servicemen followed Mrs. Barlow and Gwendolyn down the street to the church.

All I recall of my time in Manchester was my complete freedom to mix with local people. I have not a single recollection of my military activities, but sometime during the five months I was in England (I do not remember when or how), I became the Counter Intelligence Investigator for a Military Government Group of nineteen men led by a colonel. I know this because I left Manchester for Southhampton to participate in the D-Day invasion led by the same battleship *Texas* that led our armada to England.

Our team got into LCTs (Landing Craft Troops) three days after D-Day and landed on Omaha Beach on the seventh day after D-day. The beach was partially secured. That is, a trail up the hill from the beach was marked by tape, but the rest of the beach was still mined.

What I saw on day seven defies description. Seeing it on film doesn't begin to show the raw courage taken by the first wave to penetrate the massive defenses. That story has been told and is not part of my story, except that I'll never forget it.

Despite the fact that my duties were apparently of major importance, I never rose above the rank of corporal. Anyone who knows anything at all about the army knows how jealously the chain of command guards its authority. So, the corporal tells the private, the sergeant tells the corporal, etc., right up to the colonel who commands us. Not in our group. We had the colonel, a major, two captains, a first and second lieutenant, several master sergeants down to corporal. Half the non-officers were drivers and supply personnel. None of the men was assigned by rank to a team job, but rather by his skill. We had all been briefed on the War Plan which required the U.S. to recapture certain territory, the Russians, the Free French, the Belgians, etc. It didn't work out that way. The Germans contained the Russians for most of the war and only the American armies and British armies acquired ground. Because of this fact, there were far too few military government teams and our team kept switching from one army to another.

One result of our constant movement was that not one rank changed throughout the war. The ranks the team had when they were selected to form the group stayed except that I got a promotion from PFC to Tech S (Corporal) because I took a Public Safety Course in Chartres, France and gave the colonel a reason to promote me. However, I had a secretary, an interpreter, and a note that allowed me to travel anywhere during the war. As I said, rank did not translate to authority. For example, my driver was a sergeant.

§₰

Throughout my story, I have been referring to lost memory. I have been living with the idea that my memory loss was medically induced. I believe I had been privy to information best forgotten after the war. It has taken me sixty years and nearing the end of my life to wonder why I didn't try to write about the most interesting and exciting years of my life.

I now recall a quarter-ton trailer that traveled with the team through many parts of Germany. The trailer contained a giant book listing three categories of Germans — a white list, grey list, and black list. The white list contained the names of people who could be trusted to aid the cause of the allies. The grey list had the names of collaborators who might or might not be trusted. The black list contained the names of Nazis. I believe only a few members of our team were allowed to see the lists. I, as an investigator, was one of those allowed to see them. I realize now (never even thought about it before) that postwar, this information had to be destroyed and the knowledge of its existence suppressed.

At one point as we were traveling through Belgium on the way to Germany, I suddenly became ill. I remember riding, half conscious, in an ambulance traveling between rows of trees which formed a canopy over the road with flashes of sunshine coming through. I must have passed out before reaching the military hospital where I found myself when I awoke from unconsciousness. The next day (I think), an army doctor with a major's bronze leaf on his collar came to see me. He told me I had contracted encephalitis and a spinal tap had been administered that had cleared the virus. It did not seem possible to me, and I have since talked to doctors who told me that could not have happened.

While I was in the hospital, my team had moved on and I was sent to a Replacement Depot (R.D.) in Charles Le Roi, Belgium. Normally, soldiers at an R.D. were reassigned, but I believe the army had other plans for me and located my team and reunited me with my group.

The R.D. was a converted cavalry post with a high room filled with three-tiered bunks and steel shutters on the windows. It was next to a raised roadway as high as the building. It was on a road which connected Liege and Brussels and was known as "buzz-bomb lane" because the German V-1's flew overhead regularly. The V-1 was a little jet that looked like a small plane, flew about 200 feet in the air and had limited fuel. When the motor stopped, the plane went down and exploded. I saw many V-1's and saw some explode nearby. A not-so-funny incident occurred during one of these explosions in our area.

There were quite a few men waiting for reassignment playing cards or just lounging among the three-level bunk beds. When a V-1 exploded nearby, it rattled the steel shutters loudly. A young soldier asleep on an upper bunk was frightened and fell down off the bed. He picked himself up, completely disoriented and wild-eyed and started to run. Suddenly he stopped and called over his shoulder, "Going to the latrine, guys." Nobody said a word to embarrass him. We all felt the fear.

❧

Although our team's ultimate goal was to help de-Nazify Germans, and our training was toward that goal, our trip to Germany through France, Belgium, Holland, Lichtenstein, etc., was a teaching and learning experience.

One of my jobs during the combat phase of the war was to investigate crimes by the U.S. Army against German civilians. One case had to do with the rape of a German woman by two American soldiers.

I visited the woman at her house. She was about 25 years old and lived with an elderly aunt, who was not at home at the time of the alleged rape. The woman had an infant child. She claimed that the young soldiers armed with rifles knocked on her door and entered when she opened the door. The woman had taken in a large basket of laundry which had been drying on a clothesline and had the basket in the living room. She claimed that the soldiers were not menacing, but the rifles frightened her. She said that one soldier took the infant out of the room while the other spread the clothing from the basket on the floor. He raped her and the other soldier came back into the room and attacked her also.

My job was to take the evidence and turn it over to our team leader, the colonel. He was supposed to submit the evidence to the Field General of the combat troops the two soldiers belonged to. I came to realize a certain concept of leadership. My experience was that if the Commanding General was a straight-laced, tow-the-mark type, so were his troops. And if he was flamboyant, this was reflected as well. I never found out what happened to the two soldiers.

In our travels, we helped relocate the thousands of displaced persons (DPs) freed by the armies we moved with. Since our orders came directly from Supreme Headquarters, we were assigned as needed to several American armies as well as two British armies. Our team always traveled with spearheading tank armies including General Patton's. As the investigator, I had plenty to do looking for Nazi collaborators and helping the people we freed. As the only Jew on the team, the colonel thought I would be more sensitive to the needs of the DPs.

When I think about it, I try to remember how we lived during the months it took to liberate the countries we went through on the way to Germany. I know we did not sleep in tents, but can't remember the homes we occupied. Since we traveled at the tail end of spearheading tank columns, we were always in an oasis in the middle of hostile territory. We were not combat soldiers and depended on the tanks and infantry to defend us.

Our travels through Western Europe took us through Holland, France, Belgium, and Luxemburg. In each country, I was out Nazi-hunting and helping place the DPs who were not only slave laborers, but were also captured English, French, etc. — prisoners of war who were made to work.

One of the jobs of the team was to set up a temporary German government in a town. The major wanted to assign a civilian as a police officer. I found out from a person on the white list that this particular civilian was a Nazi. When I brought this to the attention of the major, he became incensed and threatened to have me court-martialed for defying his order. The next day, he came to me and apologized. We learned toward the end of the war that the major had a German girlfriend, and I learned still later that he remained in Germany after the war.

The next incident took place toward the end of the war in the period before the Battle of the Bulge, the last ditch German attempt to regain control. The spearhead tank army our team traveled with uncovered a huge factory, but the really startling thing was a living facility for hundreds of laborers under the factory. I recall that it was comfortable, though not luxurious, with kitchens, sleeping quarters, and living rooms. I'm sure there were many others, but we saw only this one.

When the Germans started to outflank our lines (The Bulge), the tank and infantry units were ordered back to re-engage the Germans. Supreme Headquarters were too busy to give us orders, so the colonel said we would have to stay behind until we got orders to move back. We were in a four-story building which was both the governor's mansion and the government offices. I remember it was called in German a "*Landratsompt*" (my spelling). We were in recently captured territory without the tank or infantry to protect us. However, our troops had taken the fight out of the enemy. We'd had enough time to get rid of the bad guys. So we holed up and waited for orders from SHAEEF (Supreme Headquarters Allied European Expeditionary Forces).

§▲

As our team traveled in Northern Germany with spearhead tank units, the tanks we were with had freed a concentration camp. I can never forget this one most horrible experience in my life. The mountain of skeletal bodies stacked against a fence, the former walking zombies! I have never since gone to see a war movie. I have no need to refresh my memory.

In the meantime, a riot broke out. The rioters were the DPs, including laborers from all the countries the Nazis conquered and conscripted for slave labor, against all conventional rules of war.

"Jules," the colonel said, "the DP's are rioting. They are destroying the flour mill and tossing sacks of flour into the street. Go out and straighten things out." The colonel was doing his job, and I, as the team investigator, would have to do mine. So, I picked up a carbine and a pistol, my American Indian driver, Morrison, with his machine gun, and my interpreter. Somewhere along the way, our tank brigades had captured a major in a German tank and a former Hungarian movie actress named "Georgie," who rode with him. Somehow, we were able to clear her; she was only trying to keep alive, and she became my interpreter because she was fluent in English and German.

Georgie, Morrison, and I, together with a German informant left the governor's mansion, where our team had holed up on the third floor, and drove a jeep to the flour mill, a mile or so away. Georgie, who had left Hungary secreted in the tank of the German Tank major, had seen so much war, she was utterly fearless, as was my driver, Morrison. I had enough fear for all three of us, but only I knew that.

When we got to the rioting mob, I found a French sergeant and a British sergeant-major. Under my instructions, they organized their people and withdrew them from the riot area.

I could easily relate to the frustration, hate, and anger toward their former captors who used them and mistreated them. The DPs were conscripts from all the countries the Germans had overrun, plus the French, English, Russian, etc., soldiers who were forced into labor.

We managed to quell the riot. The flour mill fed the DPs first, as well as the enemy— the Germans.

I was discharged from service on December 31, 1945 after three years of this journey of intrigue.

NOTE: In 1948 Jules married Pearl; they have two sons and a daughter. He first worked for a producer of advertising premiums, then moved on to a construction company that manufactured mail chutes for tall buildings. The latter supplied the training for Jules to found, along with a partner, their own business of assorted chutes – mail, debris and fire escape. After retirement in 1982, he and Pearl relocated to the west coast where their children and grandchildren resided. He became a voracious reader. Though only with the Rossmoor Writers for a brief time himself, Jules has long maintained his reputation for gregariousness and wit while escorting Pearl to the groups' social gatherings.

Honorable Discharge

This is to certify that

JULIUS S SCHWARTZ 32 709 227 TECHNICIAN FIFTH GRADE

3RD MILITARY GOVERNMENT REGIMENT

Army of the United States

is hereby Honorably Discharged from the military
service of the United States of America.

This certificate is awarded as a testimonial of Honest
and Faithful Service to this country.

Given at   SEPARATION CENTER
            FORT DIX, NEW JERSEY

Date   31 DECEMBER 1945

I Certify that this document
is a true and exact copy of
either the original or a
certified copy issued by a
public custodian of records
which I have personally examined.

Accredited Representative

CONTRA COSTA COUNTY
VETERANS SERVICE OFFICE
10 DOUGLAS DR., SUITE 100
MARTINEZ, CA 94553-4078

JILL MARTINEZ
(925) 313-1481

E. B. NELLIS
MAJOR, INFANTRY

Front of Jules' Honorable Discharge
Document supplied by author

ENLISTED RECORD AND REPORT OF SEPARATION
HONORABLE DISCHARGE

SCHWARTZ JULIUS S	32 709 227	TEC-5	M P	AUS
3RD MIL GOV REGT	31 DEC 45	SEPARATION CTR FT DIX NJ		
707 HOPKINSON AVE BROOKLYN NY	17 SEP 17	NEW YORK NY		
SEE #9	HAZEL BROWN 5-8½ 175 lbs.	1		
W X X	CLERK TYPIST 1-37.340			

MILITARY HISTORY

7 JAN 43 | 14 JAN 43 | NEW YORK NY

149 | KINGS NY | SEE #9

INVESTIGATOR 301 | NO RECORD

ARDENNES, CENTRAL EUROPE, NORTHERN FRANCE, RHINELAND
GO 33 WD 45 AS AMENDED

EUROPEAN-AFRICAN-MIDDLE EASTERN SERVICE MEDAL, GOOD CONDUCT MEDAL, WORLD WAR II VICTORY MEDAL, AMERICAN SERVICE MEDAL

NONE

16MAR44 26AUG45 14MAR44 NONE | 5 APR 44 | E T O | 17 APR 44
| 13 DEC 45 | U S A | 25 DEC 45

TEC-5

NONE

CONVENIENCE OF THE GOVERNMENT AR 615-365 15 DEC 44 AND RR-1-1 DEMOBILIZATION

NONE Military School of Public Safety, CHARTRES France

PAY DATA

24 300 100 $148.00 4.05 $304.69 J HARRIS COL FD

INSURANCE NOTICE

31 DEC 45 31 JAN 46 6.70

LAPEL BUTTON ISSUED
ASR (2 SEP 45) - 69
INACTIVE ERC FROM 7 JAN 43 TO 13 JAN 43

Julius E Schwartz | J E WHITE JR CAPT AC

Back of Jules' Honorable Discharge

JOELIE PEHANICK has been a part of the class for many years. She is one of the best writers in the class and writes a variety of stories — some moving, some thought provoking and some showing her sense of humor. She is the author of a novel, Porch Light Burning, *which depicts a Reno of 60 years ago. She reads well, capturing the nuances of each person, and this story is one she has heard in bits and pieces over many years from her husband Joe.*

THE TELEGRAMS

Joe couldn't remember the last time he was so elated. Yes, he'd just lied to the Western Union man about his age to get the job. He wasn't sixteen — what they required. But his tall-as-a-telephone-pole and skinny-as-a-dipstick frame — in fact, sometimes his ma called him 'six o'clock' — allowed him to pass for older. He was sure he'd have no trouble delivering telegrams around Scranton. After all, he'd explored every block of the town in his fifteen years. The best part of hearing he got the job was that he could start Saturday. Ma needed the money now. Sure, she got her share of ration stamps, but they did her no good without the money to redeem them. Her pots of holupki were mostly cabbage these days, and the family's sandwiches were bread and ketchup only, both homemade.

It was 1944, wartime, in a railroad and mining town that was still reeling from the Great Depression. Joe had two sisters and five brothers. The two oldest — army men — were overseas fighting. Two younger ones were in school, along with Joe. The other brother and sisters, one about to marry an army man, grasped at whatever menial jobs they could — however and whenever. His father, drinking again, wasn't working. Yes, Ma needed the money — not for clothes or gasoline — but for food and to replace the leaky roof on their old two-bedroom frame duplex.

"You'll work every day after school, eight hours on Saturday and sometimes on Sundays. OK with that?" asked the manager. He had a raspy, deep-from-the-chest voice that reminded Joe of the electric sander in woodshop at school.

"Sure," he answered, his elation building on hearing the long hours.

"You'll be called names, you know... womens' underwear, penny pincher, nickel grabber, that kind of thing." He peered at Joe with eyebrows raised, glasses reflecting a ceiling light above his desk. "You look like you can handle that."

Those aren't as bad as "dumb hunky," Joe thought to himself. But he answered with a quick, "Sure I can," then added shyly, not used to asking adults such questions, "but... womens' underwear? What... what does that have to do with anything?"

The manager grinned. "Nothin.' It's just that Western Union and women's underwear have the same first letters, and some fools decided to connect the two." He crossed one leg over his knee, leaned back in his swivel chair and answered the telephone, cradling the receiver between his ear and shoulder and scribbling on a yellow pad. Joe looked about the room, listening to the muffled sounds of the Teletype machine clicking upstairs. The place smelled of stale tobacco smoke and dust. A cobweb in one corner caught his eye; it quivered as a spider raced across to his frantic victim. A friendly robust fire crackled in a stove nearby. Scooting closer carefully, because his metal chair was rickety and dotted with rust spots, he stretched his hands to the warmth. Outside the one window there was a steady onslaught of snowflakes forming an even white shelf on the sill. One wall had a bulletin board jammed with tacked-on cartoons and notices in all sizes. From where Joe sat, the only thing he could make out was one of those war recruitment posters — the bearded man with the piercing eyes dressed in red, white and blue pointing dead on at the reader with bold letters proclaiming, "Uncle Sam Wants You." It made his thoughts jump to his brother, nineteen-year-old Paul in Europe somewhere. He'd overheard a conversation in their kitchen between his mother and sisters right after Paul got his orders. "Remember him telling us — after he went for his physical?" Ma had said. "One doctor said he was too tall, over 6'6." Another doctor came over and looked him up and down. 'Take him anyway. We need him,' he said." His oldest sister, her voice brimming with indignation, had said, "He shouldn't even be in this war!"

The image of Paul leaving Scranton was indelible in Joe's mind. The backyard of their house joined the railroad tracks where he and his brothers often gathered chunks of coal that bounced off the boxcars and ate tomatoes straight from the vine with the juice of them dripping off their elbows. But that day the whole family gathered there facing the tracks waiting to see Paul. When the troop train roared by, they spotted him for an instant, hanging out of a window from the waist up, waving and shouting madly at them, army cap in hand. Back in the kitchen they had all laughed over the scene — Paul's excitement, seeing him in uniform, thrilled that they were even able to catch a glimpse of him with the train going so fast.

The manager banged down the receiver and swiveled his chair back and forth for a moment studying the notes he'd just taken. He looked up from them reluctantly. "Ah... how about your bike? You'll be putting on a lot more miles. Can it take the beating?"

"Oh, it's a good one," replied Joe, thinking of how many times he'd had to repair it and patch tires in the last few months.

"We have a uniform, you know." He nodded toward a wall rack mounded with a row of green jackets and caps with Western Union lettering. "We'll hand you a set when you pick up your telegrams every day." The manager glanced at the bottoms of Joe's pant legs. Joe blushed; his ma had spliced wide strips of fabric on them to make them longer so his bare legs wouldn't poke out and turn blue from the cold. "We don't require uniform pants," the man added hastily. "Whatever you have will do. And when it's really cold you can just wear your own jacket." He leaned forward and squinted at Joe like an owl trying to see during the day. "One hard and fast rule to keep in your head when you're delivering: stay off the sidewalks with your bike. Streets only. Got that?"

"Yes, sir." Joe cleared his throat. Gathering courage, he put in a pitch for his buddy George getting hired too. Both being Slovak in a mainly Irish neighborhood, and laughing at the same things — nearly everything and almost nothing — had made them pals way back when they started kindergarten together. Even then Joe was nearly a foot taller than his best buddy, and the two, side by side, often generated good-natured comments like, "Here comes Mutt & Jeff again!"

"Yeah, we could use another guy. The sissies tend to quit in this cold weather," the manager said, disgust shadowing his face. He fished a thin rectangle of paper and a little draw stringed cloth pouch from his breast pocket. From the pouch, he scattered loose tobacco the length of the paper, rolled it up and carefully licked one long edge to make it stick. Joe had never seen this; he was fascinated with the fluidness of the man's motions and wondered if the tobacco was going to slide out the ends. It flared a bit when he lit up, but the cigarette held, at least on one end. "Any questions, boy?" He spat a strand of tobacco off his lip into a wastebasket.

Joe was too excited over the job and the possibility of George getting hired to come up with more conversation other than, "No. Thank you, sir."

The phone rang again, and the manager gave him a nod of dismissal. "See you Saturday at 8 sharp." He answered, "Popovich." Joe, with the lack of grace that accompanies a thundering growth spurt, unfolded from his chair cautiously so as not to tip it over. He headed for the door, giddy with planning how he'd break this colossal news to his ma. "Hold it a sec, Mike," said the manager, putting his hand over the receiver. "Son, don't you want to know what you're gonna get paid?"

"Oh… oh sure."

"Thirty-five cents an hour. Even a tip once in a while." He winked. "That's where 'nickel grabber' comes from."

§&

Joe was proud of handing his paycheck and occasional treasured tips over to his ma at the end of each week. Once in awhile, not often, she gave him back a nickel. He'd had trouble settling into the long hours. One day after school he didn't turn up for work, so Western Union sent a messenger over to his home. The humiliation of having his ma drag him out of the high school gym, where he was turning out for an unexpected empty slot on the basketball team, stifled any more thoughts of cutting work. Besides, pretty soon George got hired on. They'd each be given a stack of some twenty telegrams, and out of eyesight of the office, they'd sort them out so they could combine their routes and ride together. The two were often seen around Scranton's hills and flats, coasting with both feet on one pedal, riding 'no handle bars' with cocky looks and arms folded over their chests, hitching a free one up a steep hill by hanging on to the back of a trolley car, and pumping as fast as their leg muscles would tolerate to get home before dark. And they laughed a lot, boisterously with their heads thrown back, unrestrained, as only teenage boys can.

One below-zero Sunday, with Joe wearing socks on his hands to keep them from frostbite, and the two of them stamping their feet to ward off numbness, they had begun their sorting process when George said, "Thanks a lot, buddy."

"For what?" answered Joe.

"For calling in sick yesterday, that's what."

"It was just plain too cold. But how did you know?"

"How do you think I knew? They called ME in, you jerk. I was out there with my hands freezing to my handlebars — cause I lost my gloves — and skidding on the ice. And I couldn't blow my nose 'cause my snot was frozen — working YOUR shift. All the while I suppose you were at home toasting those 14's by the kitchen stove." Joe slapped his leg and burst into a guffaw so loud that passersby stared. The more George glared at him, the louder Joe laughed. Pretty soon his pal broke down and joined in. They danced around on the sidewalk punching each other in the forearms and shadow boxing with weaves and ducks — like they'd seen boxers do down at Town Hall when they'd sneaked in. The bong of St. Lucy's church bells announcing four o'clock sent them back to their sorting. Joe held a telegram aloft.

"I wonder what this means. The envelope's got stars." The two stared at it.

"Better ask," said George. "I'll wait here for you, OK?" Joe walked back to the office holding the envelope with the stars on it separate from the others. He returned within minutes.

"Well?" said George.

"It… the three stars mean the person has been killed in action." He took off his cap and raked through his hair with his fingers. "I'm supposed to… to stay and comfort the family after I deliver it."

"Jeez! How you gonna do that?"

"I don't know. I don't even know them. But Popovich told me that's what I had to do."

Joe gripped the telegram with the stars, his last on the route, because the address was just two blocks from his own. In front of the house he stood on the iced sidewalk, his bike propped against a tree. He watched George pedal around the corner toward home. Sky, snow and trees were shades of pewter gray around him in this limbo between dusk and night. He shivered, straightened his cap, and walked up the steps to the front door and knocked. A pretty woman, slender with a heart shaped face and long dark hair, opened it. After a quizzical glance at Joe her eyes fell on the telegram. He handed it to her, his throat too constricted to speak. She ripped it open and scanned the few pasted on words. He had never heard such a sound from anyone. It was a scream but so raw, so primal that he felt it more in his gut than heard it with his ears. He backed away from her and stumbled on the porch step, grabbing at a balustrade. Pedaling towards home as fast as possible, he couldn't tell if she was still screaming, or if they were echoes in his skull. With one hand, he steadied the bike over the slick road, and with the other, tried to brush tears from his cheeks. But they were frozen there. At home, he spoke little and ate less. The voices of his brothers and sisters seemed to blend into a kind of background chorus like what he sometimes heard on radio programs. After supper, Ma, alone darning socks by the kitchen stove, asked if he was "coming down with something." He finally told her what he'd had to do — and that, even though he was supposed to, he just couldn't think of a word to say to the lady. Ma dropped the sock she was darning into her sewing box. He stared vacantly at the needle and thread still sticking out from the toe. "Poor soul," she said. "That poor soul."

It was an early December day, and with everyone remarking on it, the below zero temperature had risen enough to allow a snowfall to mantle the city. It was also a fluke day for Joe and George; they had few telegrams, a signal to horse around before starting deliveries. They were careful to move away from the office for their shenanigans though, because the week before Joe had gotten fired. His boss had spotted him breaking that cardinal rule, biking on the sidewalk instead of the street. Ma didn't have to say a word when he, with the look of a beaten dog, muttered his news. He watched her features working for control. Muscles twitched, eyes blinked and watered, and her lips totally disappeared. Joe felt rotten. She shoved a simmering pot of rice to the back of the stove, bundled up and grabbed him by the elbow. The two trekked across town in the dark on snowy sidewalks, her to plead for his job back. And plead she did. Ashamed to hear his mother have to beg for him, he stood next to her in the Western Union office, mumbling promises not to break the company's rules again. It worked.

Now, with the few telegrams stuffed in bags in their bike baskets, he and George were having a snowball fight, ducking behind stout trees when the one would fire a packed zinger at the other. Joe had just scored a direct hit — George's face. "Hah! You think you can get away with that?" his buddy shouted.

"So what the hell do you two think you're doing?" said someone even louder. Joe knew that voice. He peeked from behind a tree and frantically brushed the snow from his uniform jersey and sock covered hands. It was Popovich standing in the middle of the sidewalk, so encased in clothing that only his face from mouth to eyebrows was exposed. Jumping on his bike, terrified and pumping vigorously past him, he called over his shoulder, "We were just leaving, sir." He didn't exhale until, mercifully, he heard the boss, still in the middle of the sidewalk, explode a huge belly laugh.

❧

Shortly after New Year's, the boys were delivering downtown. Joe was headed for the bank and George for the

Hotel Casey. "I'll meet you after in front of City Hall," Joe said. "Hey, George, if you can deliver right to the room instead of the front desk you might get a tip."

"Fat chance. You know how those bellhops fall all over each other to take it up themselves," George replied. "But I'm going to give it my best."

Joe got to City Hall first. To keep warm, he rode in tight figure eights on the street close to the curb. Still, a couple of truckers honked and glared at him so he propped the bike, dug his hands deep into his mackinaw pockets and stamped up and down on the sidewalk. George skidded up to the curb panting. "You'll never guess what happened," he said. Face flushed and cap askew, he jumped off his bike and bounced it up the curb.

"Did you get to deliver to the room?" asked Joe.

"Did I! Did I!"

"So you got a big tip?"

"Yeah – a whole fifty cents!" He stepped up close to Joe and shook his head vigorously. "But that's not the story. You won't believe this! There were no bellhops around so I went fast right up the elevator to the room and knocked. The door opens and a lady in panties and a brassiere is standing there — nothing else on!" George was still panting. "Two more ladies dressed the same were standing behind her. They all stared at me. Then they stared at the floor. I'd dropped the telegram and didn't even know it!"

"Wow!" said Joe. He pictured the scene. "Wow! Wish I'd been along. Wait'll you tell this at The Corner!"

George wiped his brow with his sleeve and stuffed his hair back under his cap. "Well, I'm sure as heck not going to tell it at the dinner table tonight."

Joe couldn't wait to get home and pass this story on to his brothers — not in front of his ma and sisters, of course. He banged through the front door and smelled the rich yeasty scent of baked bread. He knew Ma had pulled the loaves out this morning, but their aroma remained and whirled faintly around him as he made for the kitchen. But, disappointingly, none of his brothers were around. He could hear his sisters upstairs arguing about something or other, and Ma was in the kitchen alone making egg noodles on the table. They talked while she bent to her task, and he ate a couple of ketchup sandwiches. He watched her stack the rolled out dough in layers, slice evenly through them to form the pale yellow strands, then separate them for drying.

Hearing voices outside, Joe remembered about the ice rink in the field across the street. In past winters ice had formed enough for the neighbor kids to skate. That was because in summer the area was a dirt baseball field and a CCC guy* kept it pretty groomed. But two days before, a dandy thing had happened; a water pipe had burst. Before anyone could repair it the water had spread through the field and frozen, forming an even bigger and thicker rink. He smiled to himself remembering that coming home, he had walked right by it with everybody skating and hollering and hadn't even noticed because he was still thinking about George at the Hotel Casey.

"I'm going to go skate, Ma," he said, flicking crumbs off his shirt front. He'd saved up the tip money she'd passed back to him and bought ice skates in a thrift shop for twenty five cents. They were too small but the biggest he could find. Besides, no one that skated in the field seemed to have good fits. Some would stuff their skates with socks, others would have to quit because their cramped toes hurt too much; that's what usually happened to Joe.

"Haul in some more coal first," Ma called to him at the front door. He returned, filled the coal bin then crossed to the ice. It was dusk, but streetlights reflected onto the edges of the frozen field like something in a movie. He skated onto the unintentional rink. It was the best he'd ever been on, smooth and solid with the extra thickness of it. His blades sliced into the ice boldly as he joined the circle of skaters. Finding himself behind Julie, a neighbor, he tried to imitate her smooth glide.

"Hey, Joe!" someone yelled behind him. "Wait up!" He looked over his shoulder, waved and slowed down. It was his cousin Stanley who lived with his family in the second half of their duplex. Stanley arrived red-faced and puffing beside him. He grasped Joe's arm for balance.

"Hey, Stanley! You'll never guess what happened to George today." They were at the far end of the rink from the house now. Skating slowly, Joe began, "He had to deliver at… " but out of the corner of his eye he noticed the skaters closest to his house slowing, some stopping and staring at it. He left Stanley and skated down the middle of the rink. Before he reached the edge, he heard screams. They were coming from his open front door. He ripped off his skates and raced in stocking feet across the street and into the house. It was his mother and sisters screaming in the kitchen. As though punched in the stomach, one sister was doubled over hanging on Ma's arm. The other, pale as a turnip, was clutching the back of a chair. Ma, gasping, stood ramrod straight in the middle of the room. "Paul!" they were screaming. "Paul!"

"What about him?" Joe shouted. One sister pointed feebly

to the table. He picked up a telegram from on top of the drying noodles and read it. "We regret to inform you that your son Paul Pehanick was killed in action in the Battle of the Bulge on January 5, 1945... ." An older brother burst into the room yelling, "What's happened? What is it?" His eyes darted from one face to the other.

"Paul's dead!" a sister wailed.

Ma placed her hands heavily on Joe's shoulders. She closed her eyes. "Go back and skate, Joe. Go back and skate." He turned and ran past his brother and out of the house, back across the street, laced up his skates and bounded onto the rink. Again, his blades sliced through the ice but deeper this time and faster and faster. The other skaters became a blur of slow moving bundled bodies in shades of gray blending with the darkening day. Chest heaving, skinny arms pumping, he couldn't stop.

The Civilian Conservation Corps was a federal work relief program established for young men from unemployed families during the Great Depression. Among other things, the CCC is credited with planting three billion trees as part of a reforestation program designed to control the soil erosion that created the Dust Bowl.

NOTE: In 1949 Joe left Scranton with a sister for Seattle, Washington. Though not having played high school sports, he received a basketball scholarship to Seattle University, earned a B.A. there and made All American Honorable Mention. In 1955, he married Joelie, author of The Telegrams, *later beginning a 40 year career in the tire business. His greatest pride: 6 children, their spouses and 22 grandchildren. Joe wondered during that last glimpse of his brother Paul whether he would ever see him again. He scoffs at the concept of the word "closure," still treasuring Paul's life, as well as the lives of all military killed in battle.*

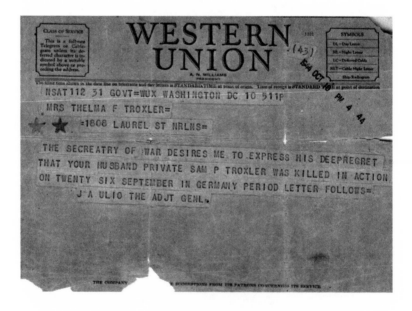

A typical telegram notifying a family of a loved one's death in combat.

From the National World War II Museum, New Orleans, La.

RUTH ROQUE-WOOD and her husband Bruce are among the more giving and affable members of the Rossmoor writers. Ruth is a talented actress and costume designer. She is currently working on a meticulously researched historical novel set in fifteenth century Spain, when Jews were ordered to convert to Christianity or leave the country.

PAPA, PLANES, AND PRISONERS

My parents, younger sister and I lived in a small California town called Soledad (Spanish for solitude) in the heart of the 90-mile-long Salinas Valley. The valley was made famous by John Steinbeck and is often referred to as Steinbeck country. His novel *Of Mice and Men* is set in Soledad. In the early 1800s the area now forming Soledad was part of Rancho San Vicente owned by Don Estaban Madras. The rancho's 19,000-plus acres were located on the east side of the Salinas River across from Soledad Mission. In his will, Don Munras instructed his wife, "Hold onto the land, and when the time is right, subdivide for a township. Give one lot for a church, one for a school, and one for a cemetery." These donated plots were the beginning of Soledad.

My parents settled in Soledad in the late 1930s when the population was a little over three thousand. The town boasted a bank, a booming dairy industry, cattle ranches and farms. I was born three weeks before the bombing of Pearl Harbor.

NOVEMBER, 1943

I was sitting in the middle of the small kitchen. The heat of the fire in the wood-burning stove felt good. It was the only source of warmth in our small two-bedroom house. The beige woven rocking chair squeaked as I slowly rocked and watched my mommy moving from the sink to the stove carrying a pot.

Mommy's so quiet, I thought, searching her face as she passed near me making her way to the icebox. Her large shining eyes quickly glanced up at the clock on the wall.

I heard my younger sister Joyce, who wasn't yet one, stirring from her nap in the next room. "Mommy, Tosie is awake." When I was younger, my attempt to say Joycie had come out Tosie, and the nickname stuck.

Mommy gave the clock another hurried look as she wiped her hands on the apron tied around her waist. She disappeared into the next room and soon reappeared with a rotund bundle. I watched Mommy give Tosie a quick peck on her dimpled cheek before placing her in her highchair by the table. Turning to me, Mommy said, "Come. Wash your hands now. Dinner is ready."

As I made my way to the kitchen sink, I asked, "Mommy, where's Papa?"

Once again she looked at the clock before answering, "I don't know. He's usually home by this time."

Mommy sat next to Tosie, and I sat on the other side of

my sister. It wasn't the same without Papa. The usual lively conversation at the dinner table was gone. If Papa were here, he'd make us laugh with his funny stories. Tonight the silence seemed very loud in my ears. Maybe, I thought, Mommy doesn't feel like talking because Papa isn't here. Instead I watched Mommy bend her head to one side as if listening for something. I tried to listen, too, but all I heard was the wind. The quiet was broken only when Tosie banged the tray of her highchair with her chubby hands. When we had finished eating, I played with her while Mommy cleared the table. I noticed that she had put aside the plate of uneaten food she had set out for Papa.

The sun disappeared behind the Santa Lucia Mountains. And still my Papa hadn't come home. Mommy switched on the radio and turned the dial to a station playing popular tunes. Soon the melody of *Amapola* filled the warm kitchen. Whenever Mommy heard this tune, she would serenade us in her strong low-pitched voice. I waited to hear her soothing voice, but tonight mommy forgot to sing!

After a little while, she said, "Girls, it's time for bed."

As I put my nightgown over my head, I knew I wouldn't hear the bedtime story about the monkeys who lived in the jungle. Only Papa knew it was my favorite. And he wasn't here to tell me about the games the monkeys played with one another.

The next morning I sat at the kitchen table waiting for breakfast. I watched Mommy move about the small kitchen banging pots and slamming cupboard doors. Tosie was calling, "Mama! Mama!" Mommy's eyes didn't look as bright as usual. And even though it was morning, she looked tired.

"Ruthie, please use your napkin and not your clothes to

wipe your hands," she reminded me. When I looked at her face, I could tell her eyes were not seeing and her ears weren't hearing me when I said, "Yes, Mommy." I reached for the napkin beside my plate.

Suddenly we heard the sound of car tires crunching on the gravel of the driveway. Mommy ran to the kitchen door and eagerly peered out. I jumped up from the table when Mommy pulled the door wide open. We expected to see Papa, but it was Aunt Connie coming through the door. Mommy's eyes got very wide.

"Good morning, everyone," Aunt Connie said. Then turning to Mommy she said, "Ambrose told us about Tony when he got home late last night. You really should get a telephone. Then I could've called you last night. I drove over first thing without giving the kids their breakfast and... "

"Tell me," Mommy interrupted, "Tell me. What's happened?"

Aunt Connie took a deep breath. "Recruiters from the draft board appeared where the men were working yesterday. They rounded up the younger ones in a truck, and Tony was one of them."

Mommy's face looked white. She raised her eyebrows and opened her mouth wide. Gripping the back of the chair, she asked, "Why?"

"If they pass the physicals, they'll be conscripted into the army!"

❧

Three days later, Papa finally came home. We were all so excited to see him. Tosie squealed. Mommy's face softened into a smile, and I couldn't stop grinning. I watched Papa embrace Mommy, and he winked at me over her shoulder. It was so good to have him home again.

"Tell us everything," demanded Mommy.

"Sammy, Rusty, Soltero and I were driven to Salinas. From there we were put on a train to San Francisco. We were among many who were undergoing physical exams. I had no way of contacting you. I hoped Connie would get word to you."

"She did, but it didn't free us from worrying. We didn't know what to think," stammered my mother.

"You know I would have gladly served in the army. When I learned Manila had been taken by the Japanese, I feared for my family there." Then holding Mommy at arm's length and looking into her eyes, he continued, "It would have meant being away from you and the girls though."

"Well, I'm glad you didn't have to leave us. What about Soltero and the others?"

"They were told to get things in order because they would be sent to Fort Ord for basic training."

"Why didn't they take you?"

"Remember that when I first arrived in the country years ago, I had been run over by a truck and almost lost my right leg?"

"Yes, you said the doctors wanted to amputate it."

"I managed to save it, but it turns out my right leg is shorter than the left one. This old injury was the reason why the army didn't draft me!"

OCTOBER, 1944

Soledad's citizens wanted to help in the war effort. The dedicated work of groups of volunteers searching the skies for enemy planes for countless hours was one way. I remember how Aunt Connie asked my mother to join. "A group of us are going to the Mission area to spot enemy planes tomorrow morning. Do you want to come along? I have an extra pair of binoculars."

"Sure," my mother said, "if I can bring the girls."

"That shouldn't be a problem. We always bring plenty of food and water. If the girls get tired, they can take a nap."

Early the next morning, Mommy, Tosie and I piled into Aunt Connie's car and headed to the Mission District, just three miles south of Soledad. Mommy had filled a large basket with food. Joyce and I were excited to be on this outing. We arrived to find that the once lush green hills had turned golden. The wide limbs of the oak trees welcomed us, offering shade from the warm October sun. The gently sloping hills made a wonderful playground. While Tosie and I chased one another until we got tired, the grown-ups searched the sky through their binoculars for planes with a red circle painted on their wings. A book with drawings and descriptions of Japanese and German planes was in their possession and a ready reference. The group of men and mostly women stood out there for hours talking, scanning and referring to the book whenever a plane was spotted.

§.

Who could have foreseen that this peaceful small town would play yet another unusual role during WWII?

The federal government had built a housing unit northeast of town on Benito Street. This housing was originally intended to shelter workers under the Guayule Emergency Rubber Project. The project involved bringing the guayule plant from Mexico and planting it in the Salinas Valley. If successful, it would provide a rubber substitute and an independent supply of domestic rubber for use in the war. At some point, the guayule experiment was considered a failure and discontinued. Now the barracks, which had originally been built to house the guayule laborers, were to be dedicated to a different purpose.

"Did you hear," said Mommy to Aunt Connie who lived in the south end of town, "that the government housing built for the *braceros* will now hold German prisoners?"

"Yes, I did. Who could have ever imagined that this would happen in Soledad?"

"Well, I certainly didn't. The *Soledad Bee* says the first group of German prisoners will arrive this weekend! This prison is too close for my peace of mind."

෧

It was a bright October morning. Both sides of Bonito Street were lined with residents standing in front of their homes. The first German prisoners to be incarcerated in the government housing and Quonset huts had arrived. I stood close to Mommy who kept looking nervously up the street. I heard the neighbors speak to one another in high pitched voices. Most of us had never seen Germans. We were there to witness the foreign detainees' arrival. Suddenly someone shouted, "Here they come!" All heads turned.

A group of 40 or so men dressed in light blue shirts were marching towards us. They were flanked by U.S. soldiers outfitted in olive green uniforms carrying rifles.

"Oh, Ruthie," said Mommy reaching for my hand as the group paraded nearer. Aside from the Swiss Italians who had settled in the area, we didn't know anyone from Europe except for the priest who had come from Spain. I could hear a few people muttering. Some yelled things I didn't understand, but most of the people watched in silence.

I felt Mommy tighten her grip. I wondered if the prisoners were scary looking, but I was afraid to look. I closed my eyes, then opened them just enough to see the blurred outlines of the approaching men. My eyes popped wide open when Mommy suddenly jerked me from the edge of the curb. I looked right into the blue eyes of a fair haired youth who quickly turned his face. As the prisoners passed, I saw that a large white "P" had been painted on the backs of their shirts.

"Ohhh, Ruthie," Mama whispered. "They're only boys!" And I saw tears roll down her cheeks.

NOTE: Ruth Roque-Wood left Soledad to attend San Francisco State during the sixties, a renowned era in the city. She married, had two children (one delivered by her physician boss), divorced, and later married Bruce. She worked for various large companies, finally retiring from Kaiser Steel in 1994. Of the war years Ruth comments, "Our family didn't lack the essentials, but my sister and I were taught to conserve at a very young age."

SOLEDAD BEE

A Home-Town Newspaper Published Weekly in the Heart of the Salinas Valley

SOLEDAD, MONTEREY COUNTY, CALIFORNIA, FRIDAY, OCTOBER 6, 1944

CAMP SOLEDAD IS NOW AN ARMY PRISON CAMP

Camp Soledad, built by the government a little over a year ago, to house Mexican Nationals used in the Guayule planting and cultivation and later expanded to include other transient field labor, has been remodeled into a prison camp. Accurate reports say it will house 500 German prisoners. They are to be brought here from Ft. Ord, location center of the Monterey County prison camp for German prisoners.

The prisoners will be under army supervision and control. Three watch towers have been constructed and a fence enclosure around the barracks has been added. Flood lights have also been installed. Some 60 army men will be located there as guards and with the cooks and servicemen the total personnel is expected to reach 100.

The prisoners will be utilized in farm work in this area and will be taken out to the ranches in the ranch owners' trucks under army guards.

The camp is expected to be ready for occupancy this weekend and the prisoners moved here from Fort Ord.

SYLVIA ROSE joined the Writers Group for help with a story of a trailer trip with her dog Meadow, but War Baby took precedence. Among other lessons, the war years taught her frugality, made it difficult to deal with loss and gave her "an awareness of her small place in the greater whole."

WAR BABY

I was born on September 12, 1939. My father always called me his little "War Baby." As a child, I felt it was a distinction that made me special, perhaps even heroic. The full significance of having been born eleven days after Hitler invaded Poland, igniting World War II, has been revealing itself over the years, often unexpectedly, punctuating my life with memories and insights— similar to looking at a fading, yet familiar photograph and discovering details unnoticed before.

We lived in Santa Barbara, California where my father taught German and Art History at Santa Barbara College, later to become the University of California at Santa Barbara. Born in Switzerland, he had immigrated to America as a young man. When the war began, he was too old to enlist in the military, but wanting to participate somehow in the war effort, he joined the American Red Cross, shifting quickly to the International Red Cross where his linguistic skills — he spoke five languages — could be well used.

During the long years of the war, my mother and I saw him just two short weeks a year, sometimes even less. When he did come home he brought wonderful gifts! Chocolates from Switzerland, a delicately hand-embroidered dress for me, a blouse for my mother from Romania, colorful fabrics, costumed dolls, and a caravan of hand-carved olive wood camels from the Middle East. Exciting, exotic things I could show to my friends proving I really did have a father!

However, not all that he brought home was wonderful. One night I was awakened by loud noises, like firecrackers. Unable to sleep well, my father had become angry at the screeching of some mating cats and had shot at them blindly in the dark with the gun he now carried with him. My mother and several of our neighbors were terrified.

There was, also, the contents of a rumpled brown bag. Passing out gifts during another visit home, my father handed me the bag out of which tumbled a pair of short, baggy black pants, a khaki shirt and a funny looking black hat with a dangling tassel. It was the uniform children wore in fascist Italy. He told me to put them on.

When I look at the photo he took of me that day, my right arm raised in an unfamiliar salute, I notice my eyes are shut. I remember feeling a sense of confusion tinged with shame. I felt there was something bad about those clothes with their colors, so dark and sinister. Perhaps he thought they were merely a harmless souvenir or a funny costume appropriate for Halloween. I'll never know.

To mitigate the agony of his many departures, and, we

hoped, to insure his safe return, he and I developed a secret ritual we performed faithfully just before he stepped aboard the train. He would take a stick of Wrigley's chewing gum from his pocket and tear it halfway through. Then he would offer it to me, and I would tear it the rest of the way. As we put our halves in our mouths, chewing slowly, tasting the fresh sweetness, he kissed me goodbye. Then he stepped aboard the slowly moving train that was once again pulling him away from me. I still remember standing on the platform, chewing my half piece of gum, waving, crying, and watching until I could no longer see his waving arm.

My earliest memories are of limited supplies of certain foods and gasoline, precious ration books, Victory Gardens, and feeling my mother's pride whenever she fulfilled a task that was in support of the war effort. For example, we diligently collected all our tin cans for recycling. After both ends had been removed, I stomped on the cans making them as flat as possible. Then, without cutting my fingers, I carefully slid the ends inside. Once a week my mother allowed me to help her mix a small packet of dark orange powder into a block of soft white stuff, turning it the color of butter.

"Real butter is for our boys fighting overseas," she explained.

On certain evenings I couldn't interrupt her as she sat unmoving, facing our large, floor-model radio listening to a man's strong, resolute voice. When I grew a bit older I learned that the voice belonged to President Franklin Roosevelt. His "fireside chats" conveyed an unfaltering conviction that we could and would win the war. So, when I came home from school one day to find my mother crying, something she rarely did, I, too, was filled with a sense of loss and confusion.

I didn't understand what it meant, but I knew something bad had happened. His reassuring voice was gone forever, and my mother was uncertain about when, or how, the war would end.

I remember large posters in store windows commanding us to buy war bonds and life-size cardboard images of a white bearded man dressed in red, white and blue pointing a finger at me saying, "Uncle Sam Wants You!"

"Who is Uncle Sam?" I asked my mother.

"Oh, he is President Roosevelt telling us to do our part to help win The War," she explained. "That's why you turn off the lights when you leave a room and eat all the food on your plate. You mustn't waste a thing, Sylvia."

To this day, I can't leave food on my plate, and I taught my four children not to put more food on their plates than they could comfortably consume. I also remember streetlights painted black on the sides facing the sea and periodic blackouts. Sometime after Pearl Harbor, a Japanese submarine shelled an oil storage depot at Gaviota, a few miles north of Santa Barbara. After that, I felt an increased sense of apprehension amongst the adults around me.

Whenever possible during those long war years, my mother would pack our 1937 Buick with home-baked goodies, gifts, and me and drive north on Highway 101 to San Francisco to join her mother and unmarried sister for Thanksgiving or Christmas. We always stopped at a favorite place near King City for our picnic lunch and a well-earned stretch. Another much anticipated stop on our route was Camp Roberts, a busy staging base for troops in transit. There was no public transportation nearby, so many soldiers stood on the highway thumbing rides north and south, trying to get home on leave, especially during the holidays. My mother felt it her duty to pick up a soldier and help him get home to his family. I remember a sense of happy anticipation as we stopped to pick up a soldier. It was always more exciting to hear stories first hand as we traveled than it was to watch black and white Movietone Newsreels in a darkened theater.

However, I'll never forget the last time we stopped to pick up a soldier. He was standing apart from the others thumbing their way north, a bulky duffle bag at his feet. When Mother pulled over and opened the trunk, he tossed the heavy bag inside, then slid into the passenger's seat. I was perched on top of our suitcases and packages behind the front seat in a kind of nest Mother had created for me with extra blankets and a pillow. We introduced ourselves and stated our destinations. He, too, was headed for San Francisco. He said he'd been fighting in Europe but would be going to the Pacific after the holidays. We talked for awhile, then he became quiet.

After several moments he spoke slowly, softly, warning my mother to never again pick up hitchhiking soldiers. "I'm okay, ma'am, but a lot of guys aren't. They've seen too much war, and a woman like you, traveling alone with a little girl, might not be safe."

I didn't understand what he meant, but my mother did. "Thank you," she said. Then, turning her head to look at him, she added softly, "I never thought of that."

We never again stopped to pick up a soldier. I hated passing Camp Roberts after that. Fear and mistrust had replaced the innocent sense of joy I had felt as we approached waiting soldiers. That distant war had inflicted another permanent wound.

Unlike Santa Barbara, San Francisco was a big city, and

it had many mysterious places we were not allowed to go. Uniformed guards with large guns slung over their shoulders prevented unauthorized entrance into the Presidio, onto Treasure Island just off the Bay Bridge, and the huge Naval Air Station on Alameda Island where my uncle worked as a civilian machinist. From the big bay window in my grandmother's flat on Vallejo Street, I watched many ships coming and going across the great bay. She taught me to distinguish between tankers, freighters and troop transports. But the ones that made her sad were the great white ships with large red crosses painted on their sides.

"Those ships are bringing home our young men hurt in the war," she told me. I would focus her old binoculars on the decks of those ships hoping to see one of those soldiers.

I was often reminded of how fortunate I was compared to "the starving children in Europe." In one of my father's letters from Italy, he told of an orphanage filled with hungry, frightened children. Christmas was coming, and there would be no presents for them. I had two or three dolls and both my parents were alive. I dressed my favorite doll in her best dress and gave her to my mother to send to the orphanage. My father was pleased to give the doll to one of those little girls.

VE and VJ Days were very exciting, even for a five-and-a-half year old in small town Santa Barbara! Whistles blew, the Mission bells rang nonstop and people gathered downtown along State Street and around the courthouse to hug and be happy together. We had been taught in school to respect our country and its flag, so when I saw cars dragging red and white and red, white, and black flags behind them on the ground I asked why.

"We've won the war!' I was told. "Those are the flags of our enemies! They deserve to be dragged in the dirt!"

Sirens and jubilation ended that long time of apprehension. It also meant my father, that stranger in uniform, who appeared briefly each year bringing exotic gifts and who arrived and departed in terrifying bursts of steam at the train station, would soon come home to stay. No more wrenching separations, not knowing if we'd ever see him again.

With the war over, we thought my father would return home and stay. But he did not. He remained in Europe taking a post with the League of Red Cross Societies in Geneva.

In 1948, my mother and I traveled to Switzerland to join him. Our ship, the SS New Amsterdam, landed in Rotterdam, The Netherlands' main seaport, on September 11, 1948. My father met our ship.

On the drive to our hotel he pointed out how quickly, miraculously even, the Dutch had cleared their major harbor which had been savagely damaged and blockaded with sunken ships by the retreating Nazis. We could still see the jagged walls of bombed out buildings and tank abutments that remained in place in the countryside. Signs with skulls and cross bones warned of dangerous, undetonated bombs and shells.

Our hotel was on the outskirts of the city and had once been a lovely private home. It had also been a Nazi officers' billet. Two guard houses still stood menacingly on both sides of the entry door. There was a large lake behind the hotel dotted with many beautiful white swans.

The next day was my ninth birthday. At my place on our breakfast table I found a small pair of painted wooden shoes with stiff leather straps. A few sweets were tucked inside. They were a gift from the woman running the hotel. They had belonged to and had been worn by her daughter. I have them still.

Upon our arrival in Geneva a few days later, my father was devastated by the news that his colleague and friend, Count Bernadotte, a Swedish diplomat attempting to facilitate a peaceful settlement between the Palestinian Arabs and the Jewish settlers in Palestine, had been assassinated by a terrorist.

During those years in Geneva, there were several occasions when I heard survivors of the war describe some of their experiences. One evening, a friend of my father's told how she and her husband and daughter had to flee their home and country hastily. They were to be led by the underground on foot over the Alps to safety in Switzerland. But their daughter was too young to make the journey with them; she might cry and give them away. The mother told of packing her little girl into a crate, giving her enough food and milk to last a few days. She was told not to cry or make a sound. She was to be delivered to a train depot across the Swiss border and there her mother and father hoped they would find her. The mother said she did not know whether she would ever see her daughter again. After the parents made it safely over the mountains, they went straight to the train station. They found their daughter sitting on top of her box, safe and sound!

We lived in Switzerland for two years, until the outbreak of the Korean War in 1950. My mother had never liked living in Geneva and was terrified that World War III would trap her in Europe.

By then I was quite aware of the Holocaust. I had seen photographs taken in the death camps. I was also aware of the devastation the war had wreaked across Europe and the

Pacific. I began to realize how different my experiences of the war had been from those who had suffered and endured it for nearly six years.

Growing up in picturesque, safe Santa Barbara did not shield me from experiencing uncertainty, the pain of loss at a very young age, nor from having to learn to live in the aftermath of a terrible war. Conversely, however, I can't remember a time in which I felt a greater sense of belonging or of an eagerness to help in a great cause in whatever way I could. I believe my abiding sense of patriotism has its roots in having been born a "War Baby."

NOTE: After graduating from high school in Marin County, California, Sylvia earned a BS in nursing, married, divorced, and raised four children, one adopted from Taiwan. Her nursing positions have been diverse: UC Berkeley Student Health Service, Medical Phone Advice for Kaiser, Club Med in the Bahamas. A convert to Reform Judaism, she lived in Israel for five years and traveled extensively.

A U.S. Government World War II poster.

From the Northwestern University Library

*SHIRLEY BARSHAY, barely tall enough for the podium and with an infinite variety of lovely long neck scarves, read her work with a slight New York accent. A journalist since the 1940s, she never gave up writing — consistently in the nonfiction genre. Her work was beautifully structured, concise, and most often carried a social message, though she deviated from that theme for a poignant* San Francisco Chronicle *piece on losing her and her husband's home in the historical Oakland fire of 1991.*

FROM THE RADIO IN
THE KITCHEN

MONDAY, AUGUST 6, 1945

The small country house was surrounded by rolling fields. Like other old houses in town, its plain whiteness had been sparked with bright green shutters. Off to one side was a woodworking shop, flanked by lumber stacked for weathering. A rattletrap car stood in the dirt driveway. High hedges screened everything from passersby on the Carversville Road, which snaked out of the little town of New Hope, Pennsylvania, about an hour north of Philadelphia.

George Nakashima, a wood worker, his wife Marion, and their three-year-old daughter Mira, lived in the house.

I was there that day in August gathering material for a proposal to the *Ladies Home Journal*. The *Journal* ran a feature called *How America Lives*, profiling interesting families. It seemed to me the Nakashimas qualified.

I was invited to stay for supper. There would be a couple of other guests in addition to Marion's sister, Thelma, and their father, Mr. Okajima, who enjoyed cooking and was going to be chef that evening.

I had come to know the Nakashimas through my job as a writer for the War Relocation Authority in Washington, D.C. The family, including Thelma and Mr. Okajima, were among the 110,000 persons of Japanese ancestry who had been evacuated from West Coast states after Pearl Harbor.

From their home in Seattle, the Nakashimas went eventually to the Minidoka Relocation Center in Idaho. A year and a half later they "relocated" to New Hope — tentatively at first, then permanently.

George Nakashima had impressive training as an architect, but his first love was wood. For him, the creation of furniture with lasting beauty was, as he said, "Like giving trees a second life." His reputation in the design world was spreading.

I remember sitting in the low-ceilinged living room, talking and taking notes. The feeling that came quickly was serenity.

The windows of the old house were small and hewn out of thick walls. Shoji panels covered the glass, giving the room cool diffused light. On the deep sills were twists of petrified wood, mementos of Minidoka. The walls were whitewashed and sanded smooth, shading from white to gray with unexpected tones of yellow. The furniture, built mostly with simple hand tools, was natural teak, gray-brown with undertones of yellow. I remember being fascinated by the low gracefulness of the coffee table. It seemed to float. There was no bright color. An ordinary room had been given perfect balance.

Thelma and her father arrived from Philadelphia. Mr. Okajima, 77, was teaching Japanese in an army training program at the University of Pennsylvania. Thelma was a journalist and had started an affectionate, informal biography of the family. By 1942 she had written *The First Chapter In The Life of Little Mira*. She had promised me a copy. That afternoon she kept her promise.

The little book was typed on blue paper, illustrated with Thelma's line drawings and bound with string. It was dedicated to Mr. Okajima: "I dedicate this chapter in the life of Little Mira to a 13-year-old Samurai lad who stood before the Stars and Stripes waving in the breezes of Nagasaki as he listened to the words of his teacher, "This flag stands for Justice, Liberty and Equality," to the idealistic young man who came to the United States in 1892 to seek a true democracy, and to the oldest of our clan in the United States, Granddaddy Okajima, whose courage and fortitude have put many of us to shame, and whose faith in his ideals has remained like a burning flame in a world grown black with chaos and confusion... ."

Thelma was the stormy one. As she wrote in Mira's little story, she said "bad words" when she was angry. With her Eurasian features, fair, freckled skin and auburn hair, Thelma was evidence that the late Mrs. Okajima had been Dutch and French.

After a bit the last two guests arrived. One was Mrs.

Antonin Raymond, wife of the architect for whom George had worked in Tokyo from 1935 to 1937. The other guest was a young Marine who may have been a nephew of Mrs. Raymond. He had crutches and one empty pants leg. He had lost the leg in the battle for Iwo Jima.

That fragment of time remains like a scene in a play. The Nakashimas were in New Hope because they had been uprooted by the virulence of prejudice inflamed by the war on everyone's mind. The young Marine with an empty pants leg did not seem to see the Nakashimas as an extension of the enemy. The serenity of the setting grew out of the enemy's tradition of trying to express beauty in the utilitarian surroundings of everyday life.

Supper preparation was underway with the familiar homey sounds of dishes clattering and quick cutting on a wood block. Suddenly everyone was pulled into the kitchen to listen to the words from the radio, a statement by President Harry Truman:

"We are now prepared to obliterate more rapidly and completely every productive enterprise the Japanese have above ground in any city. We shall completely destroy Japan's power to make war... The fact that we can release atomic energy ushers in a new era in man's understanding of nature's forces... ."

I remember silence. The silence of people trying to comprehend what had happened in Hiroshima. Thelma broke the silence with some of her bad words.

We didn't know what lay beneath the boiling mushroom cloud seen by those who dropped the bomb and sped away. We couldn't know that three days later another bomb would be dropped.

The second bomb would fall on the city where Mr. Okajima grew up and dreamed about going to the United States, Nagasaki.

Epilogue: George Nakashima died in June, 1990 at the age of eighty-five. Perhaps his most poignant legacy is a free-form altar carved in English walnut. He called it an "Altar of Peace." Completed in 1986, it stands at the foot of the nave in the Cathedral of St. John the Divine in New York City.

NOTE: Shirley Barshay, born in Reading, Pennsylvania in 1917, began her career and true love of writing as a copy writer for Mademoiselle Magazine *in New York City. She became active in Democratic politics and moved to Washington D.C. where she met her husband, George, who was serving in the war. It was in Maryland, by now with three children, that she started decades of freelance writing, even interviewing Eleanor Roosevelt. She considered running for Congress. The family moved to California in 1965 where she resided for forty years. With her family at her side, Shirley died at home in Beaverton, Oregon at age 90.*

Tule Lake Japanese internment camp near Newell, California from 1942 to 1945.
National Archives & Records Administration (NARA)
College Park, Md.

IRMHILD EPSTEIN says that during the deprivation of the war years she was sustained by nurturing, giving friendships and the conviction that talent, perseverance and personality would prevail. She credits the Writers Group with "providing a forum for discipline and structure and learning to organize my thoughts."

WOLF WHISTLES AND LOOTING

ALTENBURG, GERMANY, 1945

I had turned fifteen in February. "Mutti! Mutti!" I ran into the kitchen, flushed with excitement. "I saw a lot of people all over town with carts full of food, and they told me there's lots more. All I have to do is get it! I'm going!"

"Oh no, you're not going out there, you understand?" My mother yelled, anger and concern in her voice, which I dismissed as usual. It was much, much later, when my own daughters were fifteen that I came to understand her concern. But at that moment, I was determined.

"Oh, I'm going, Mutti. Just think, real butter, canned meats, and coffee, real coffee, not ersatz! Wouldn't you like that?" I asked, knowing her penchant for real coffee, not the only available, unpalatable brew, commonly known as "*ersatzkaffee*" — a mixture of ground roasted rye or barley and acorns.

I knew she would stop yelling for a split second. But it was long enough for me to run out the door and down the curved wooden stairway, skipping two steps at a time, and out the old entrance door into the yard, where my brother's bike stood leaning against the wall. It was a boy's bike, with a big bar in the middle, but my brother was still away in the war. Nobody knew where, as normal circumstances had ceased to exist. So, in the meantime, the bike was mine.

I swung myself across the bar and raced through the old cobblestoned yard, out through the huge front door, a door that had once seen horse-drawn coaches roll through its wide-open wings. From there I flew down the hill of Schmöellnische Strasse, around the corner, down Moritz Strasse, passing beautiful old classical buildings dating back to the middle of the 1500's (that's before Bach's time!). But those fine points had no meaning for me as I was bumping across the cobblestones of our marketplace, going a bit slower, and then uphill at Sporenstrasse. There I had to push the bike, passing Altenburg's elite shopping and fashion houses, now pitifully empty of goods after six years of war and deprivation. There were ration cards for everything: shoes, clothes, and of course, food. Ladies' shoes, by the way, only came with wooden soles, which were cleverly cut into three parts, so they moved with your foot when walking. There was no leather for shoes.

I passed my old Bartholomaei Church where I was baptized. This venerable, sturdy building had seen much of history in its seven hundred years of existence, most famously, the rebel monk, Martin Luther, performing a marriage ceremony there between another monk and his bride. Its tower was destroyed during the invasion of marauding Hussitt Tribes. It was rebuilt with four stone angels around the top four sides to guard it against future catastrophes. It must have worked as it is still standing. As a six-year-old, I had played house with my dolls in the church niches, pretending they were my own rooms. The church was very close to the back entrance of the house where I was born and lived until we moved when I was seven.

Reaching the top of Sporenstrasse, I turned into Burgstrasse with a sigh of relief, because it was downhill from there on. I swung myself across the old boy's bar again and started flying, but the sight I encountered gave me such a jolt, that I nearly fell off the bike! It couldn't have been more bizarre or incongruous against the backdrop of my old church. American soldiers, rifles at their hips, were coming towards me, up the hill on the sidewalks of both sides of Burgstrasse. They marched in single file, kind of lumbering along in their khaki uniforms, their shirts loosened, and their helmets askew. And I was racing down the hill on my bike, right through the middle of the American soldiers, dirndl skirt and pigtails flying in the wind, unable to stop, even if I had wanted to! My God! This was the enemy invading our town, and there I was, alone on a bike! Oh, Mutti, I thought, why didn't I listen to you?

But strangely enough, I wasn't really afraid of these guys, especially when they started whistling at me, one group after another, all the way down the hill. I had never been whistled at before, but instinctively I knew it was some kind of male approval. The German boys I knew would never have shown such "crude" behavior. But I kind of liked it, and somehow I knew these guys wouldn't harm me. Today I wonder what those soldiers must have thought of this brazen teenager on a bike as they were about to occupy a pretty, old German town, whose buergermeister, wisely, thank God, had hung a big white flag on the *rathaus* (town hall) balcony.

Well, the soldiers had their business, and I had mine. And we didn't bother each other. Just a few more streets, and I was already anticipating my shopping bags filled with food such as we hadn't seen in years! We had existed mostly on barley or potato soup, peels and all, field greens, an occasional cabbage or rutabaga, onions, and sometimes bacon, which Mutti got from some farmer by bartering away our fine china, crystal, etc. Or she ingratiated herself by helping out, sitting in the kitchen, talking to the farmer's wife, or darning socks or mending clothes, sheets or whatever for them. Everything was mended, nothing thrown away. When her bags were filled, she had to walk miles back home, toting those heavy food bags. Buses? There were none. We children, even Pa, would greet her with loud cries of joy at the door, "What did you get? Show us! Unpack!"

Thank you, Mutti. We didn't say thank you enough, selfish kids that we were. Thank you for getting us through the war, Mutti. Thank you.

Next, as clear in my memory as if it had happened yesterday, there it was before me, the goal of my whole wild journey — The Depot! Its huge doors were wide open. People were scrambling, filling bags and hand carts, throwing food stuffs in teamwork with each other. Crackers, candy, coffee beans were littered all over the street. It was chaos, but I didn't care. I was quite anxious to join in the melee.

Then it happened. The huge doors closed. American soldiers had appeared and stood guard before them, rifles visible. No shots were fired. The crowd dispersed and order was restored. I stood there is utter disbelief, disappointed to the core. I probably cried. I don't know. Someone, taking pity on me, handed me a few cans of something from their stash. At least I didn't go home empty handed.

It occurred to me much later that I was involved in looting, and that there could have been riots, arrests or even shootings. Young and naïve, I just didn't know better. We were now under American occupation. But these Americans were so carefree, easy going and, gosh, so well fed! The jeep, always parked in front of the *rathaus*, was now occupied by a gum-chewing soldier, casually slumped back in his seat, relaxed, looking half asleep, certainly not threatening. One had to like these guys. They were so cool.

But alas, it didn't last. Churchill and Roosevelt, who was already sick, gave Papa Stalin a huge part of the eastern section, when they partitioned Germany like a pizza. The Americans withdrew from our town, and in came the Russians. We adjusted. The war was over. We had survived, for now.

We couldn't foresee that forty years of communism would separate us from the affluent West, plunge our lives into ruin all over again, and the world would be suspended in anxiety and fear. The Cold War had begun. But that's another story.

NOTE: Irmhild Epstein graduated from art school in Erfurt, Germany, as a silversmith, though her scholarship was withdrawn due to her anti-Communist leanings. Her trade wasn't needed in such a war torn country, but she found employment in a Stuttgart jewelry store. There she met her future husband, immigrated to New York City, and had three children. A widow now, she summers in New York, winters in Rossmoor close to two daughters, the golf course and her art.

Printed in the United States
215406BV00002B/1/P

9 780977 468911